Starting to Write

Step-by-step Guidance to Becoming an Author

D0313948

Studymates academic books

Algebra: Basic Algebra Explained
Better English
Better French
Better French 2
Better German
Better Spanish
British History 1870-1918
Chemistry: chemistry calculations explained
European History
Genetics
Hitler & Nazi Germany
Lenin, Stalin and Communist Russia
Mathematics for adults
Organic Chemistry
Plant Physiology
Poems to Live By
Poetry
Practical Drama
Shakespeare
Social Anthropology
Study skills
The Academic Essay
The English Reformation
The New Science Teacher's Handbook
The War Poets
Understanding Maths
Warfare

Studymates Writers Guides

Kate Walker's 12-Point Guide to Writing Romance
Starting to Write
The Business of Writing
Writing Crime Fiction
Writing Historical Fiction
Writing How to books
Writing Travel
Writing Tv Scripts

Studymates Post-Graduate Guides

Your Masters Thesis
Your PhD Thesis

Many other titles in preparation

Helping You to Achieve

Step-by-step Guidance to becoming an Author

Rennie Parker

Studymates

© 2007 by Rennie Parker
additional material © 2007 Studymates Limited.

ISBN: 978-1-84285-093-0

First published in 2007 by Studymates Limited.
PO Box 225, Abergele, LL18 9AY, United Kingdom.

Website: http://www.studymates.co.uk

Typeset by Vikatan Publishing Solutions, Chennai, India
Printed and bound in Great Britain by Baskerville Press

Contents

Introduction

The first thing you have to realise is that writers come in all shapes and sizes and temperaments. You don't have to be a certain type of person; you just have to be you, with an involved interest in stories and words. There are writers with demanding families, no qualifications beyond secondary school, or a chequered history of awful jobs at the bottom of the economic heap. There are writers from privileged backgrounds, with so much spare time that becoming a writer was the only way to fill it. There are one-book wonders and ten-volume epic writers, all of whom will have started out with the same questions as you: 'Where do I start?' and 'What shall I write?'

Some people decide they are writers at the age of nine, and simply keep going; others make a conscious decision in mid-life or after retirement and find that their new interest unexpectedly takes off. Many will labour for years and never achieve a publication in their lifetimes – although this book is designed to minimise the likelihood of that ever happening to you.

You must be interested in creative writing otherwise you wouldn't have picked up this book. But, like everyone else at the start, you may also be beset with fears and all kinds of denials. 'Am I good enough?' 'Isn't the market saturated already?' and 'I never seem to have enough time!' are just three of the usual worries I hear from students at the start of their work. It's true, you may have to put in years of effort before having a major breakthrough; and this book will not attempt to play down the difficulties and drawbacks. On the other hand, creative writing is one of the most fulfilling and rewarding experiences anyone can have. If your aims are realistic and your strengths are developed, this book can help you on the way to success.

Furthermore, this book can help in many instances where courses and workshops can't. You always have the information at your fingertips, you can proceed at your own pace, and the cost is minimal. You can take it anywhere and work through some of the suggestions again; and there's no tutor announcing 'time up' after an hour of frantic effort. Above all, you will save a huge amount of money.

Before you embark on that expensive correspondence course, the residential week, or the special writers' weekend in another part of Europe ask yourself: is it really necessary? If you are serious about starting to writ what is there to stop you from beginning this weekend, right now, or duri your next lunch break? Do you need to spend £500 or more in order to describe yourself as a writer? Of course not. Spend the money on a genuine holiday instead. You'll feel better, and the raw material you'll gain will be far more exciting than anything found in a classroom. Your life as a writer starts now, today, with that pencil at the bottom of your bag and the unused diary you got for Christmas.

Plenty of people want to become writers but they never actually start. It remains a dream, or they imagine themselves as writers without ever committing anything to paper. They are always 'thinking about it' or 'projects are at the planning stage'. Avoid this kind of self-deception, because it fools nobody after a while. Moreover, avoid such types if you meet them at writers' events. They'll waste your time and they can't help you, no matter how amusing, knowledgeable or influential they might seem on the surface.

Making words happen is scary at first, and you'll make mistakes – so it's worth remembering the following points:

> ➤ Be prepared to write badly at first.
> ➤ Be prepared to have half-finished and abandoned works in your files.
> ➤ A half-finished piece is better than one that never begins.

Now write these headings on a fresh sheet of paper:

Why I want to Write   **What's Stopping Me**

Take fifteen minutes to consider these headings, listing whatever springs to mind, no matter how banal or silly they sound. Mine at the age of eighteen would have looked something like this:

Why I want to Write	What's Stopping Me
I like acting and performing but the school plays were ubbish	People don't take me seriously
	There's no support
ple say I'm good at English	Don't know what to write about
rhyming verse easy	Don't know any writers
d rigid and nothing ns.	I'm worried about employment.

night have similar statements – in fact, my 'what's stopping
have remained the same up until regular publication began
your list in a safe place (a folder for all your loose sheets is

advisable) and when you have worked through this book, take it out. Has anything changed since then? Which line entries are no longer true?

Confidence is all it takes; that, and the realisation you've got nothing to lose by acting on your impulses and dreams. Age should not be a barrier either. For every wunderkind who achieves a book while still at school, there's a septuagenarian bursting into print with a shocking memoir or a delicate first collection of poetry. It's as well to remember that longevity as a writer is not necessarily linked to age.

All that matters is the drive to write and the courage to make it happen – and the questions 'Why write?' and 'why me?' can easily be answered with 'Why not?' and 'Because you're unique, too'. And despite what cynical book-people might say about overloaded markets and too many writers, new writers join the ranks of the published every year.

Since this handbook is designed to start you writing and support your aims, I will not be mentioning academic principles or typical critics' issues like 'what is literature' and 'what is creativity'. That's because college-style discussions won't help at this stage; all they will do is foster an over-analytical tendency and too much caution before you are committing words to paper. Always:

Write first. Panic later.

Now ask yourself these questions

Are you excited about the prospect of writing?

Do you already keep a journal, or relate the day's events to your family in a way which makes them listen?

Do you enjoy writing letters, and holiday postcards are never big enough?

If you spend several days without writing anything, do you notice?

Are you amused by puns, word-games, out-of-the-way factoids and information?

Are stories already part of your life, whether told to you, or made up by you?

If the answer is yes to more than two of the above, it's likely that you already have enough motivation. There's every reason why you should write; because new talent is always needed, people always want to be entertained, and even a small self-published booklet could mark a journey of personal discovery and self-fulfilment.

Note

Playwrights need more specialised guidance than I can provide here, because contemporary drama involves more team working and third-party input than the usual writer-plus-keyboard combination. But the qualities needed for good storytelling and correct writing are found in all branches of literature, and you might find some of my chapter sections helpful. For those engaged in screenwriting, I can recommend Steve Wetton's *Writing TV Scripts* (Studymates). Meanwhile, potential radio dramatists can get off to a great start by looking at the BBC writers' room website (see bibliography). Script formatting and current requirements can be downloaded direct, saving you a lot of time and effort.

Rennie Parker
rennieparker@studymates.co.uk

Where Do I Start?

One-Minute Overview

This chapter is designed to encourage the habits which make the process of writing easier. At the end of these pages you should have a growing quarry of material that you can draw upon whenever you get stuck in the future. You'll learn a few do's and a few don'ts; how not to alienate your family; and will come to realise that writing is adaptable to your particular circumstances. You will also complete, under guidance, your first image-based poem. First though, you have to look at what you should do before starting to write.

Reading

Now, be honest with yourself. How much do you read? If your sofa is covered with half-read novels face-down, and there's always a book stuffed in your locker at work, good. If the last thing you read was a shopping catalogue three weeks ago ... not so good. Writing depends on your love of narrative, images, and words. As King Lear says: 'Nothing will come of nothing'. So if you don't read, it's unlikely that your first attempts at writing will have the flow, sentence structure and interest levels which avid readers have taken in naturally through their personal history of reading.

Whether it's 'chick-lit', war novels, Harry Potter, or economic history, you must pick up material and read. This is particularly true in the case of new poets – because it's not unusual to meet the combination of a beginner poet who writes by the yard but cannot name a single contemporary poet, or any poem, that they enjoy. Ignorance is not bliss – on the contrary:

> ➤ You'll repeat common mistakes (wooden characters, poor grammar).

> ➢ You may duplicate the plots of well-known stories.
> ➢ You'll waste time on ideas which have been written to greater effect elsewhere.
> ➢ You'll remain an outsider when you should be an insider.

You can save yourself the agony, and this lack of awareness, by appreciating what literature has to offer. Keen readers are already one step ahead: even if they are unused to writing. If you don't possess a library card, obtain one this week. It should be at the top of your To Do list.

Don't worry if you hated English at school. The novels and poems used in exams are guaranteed to put you off certain authors for life. Teachers have to teach what is on the curriculum, not what is fun, easy or exciting. You are no longer forced to like the recommended classics; it doesn't matter if you couldn't understand a word of Shakespeare or Dickens or both back then. Biographies and autobiographies, popular history and straightforward literary studies will give you plenty of characters and insights. If you definitely know which genre you want your writing to fit into, collect examples from the leading authors in your field and get stuck into them.

Becoming a Critic

Start to look at literature critically.

> ➢ Is it an interesting book?
> ➢ What was good or bad about it?
> ➢ How could you improve that book?
> ➢ What was missing?

Recall the last book you have read, and on a separate sheet of paper, write your responses as honestly as you can, using the guidelines supplied above. If it was a fiction book, what kinds of events would you include in a sequel? If it was a non-fiction book, did you meet any interesting characters or learn anything new?

From now on, begin a **reading record**. It can be as formal or informal as you like – a designated notebook or loose sheets – but keep all the pages on the subject together. Provide the title and the period when you read the book; note down your spontaneous responses and any criticisms. Such records help you to remain a regular writer when working on fresh ideas is impossible. You might find your style of criticism changing over a period of time, as you become more involved in the art of writing. You might also find the following exercise helpful.

Desert Island Books

On a separate sheet of paper, list eight books or collections which have influenced you or made a significant impression – include anything read since childhood. Beside each entry, list what these books have done for you; it could range from 'it was the funniest thing ever' to 'it enabled me to survive'. Taking the most important statement, expand this into a paragraph of at least five sentences, encapsulating the value of this book in your life – what it showed you, what you learnt, how entertaining it was at the time.

Desert Island Books can be turned into a game with others – you might find that people begin arguing for the superiority of their favourite book! Events hosts at literary festivals often interview authors using this outline as a peg to secure their discussions.

Now, find out more about the authors whose works have impressed you. Nearly all of them will have website entries, if not full-scale biographies available.

Why should you read about authors? Because you will pick up a great many writing tips in the process. The following one, from Ernest Hemingway, has been recommended to many students – and they tell me it's rather good:

> *End the day's work on a half-finished sentence. When you return the following day, you will automatically continue from where you left off.*

Minor forms of writer's block and 'where do I start' worries are abolished at a stroke. Thanks, Ernest!

Keeping a Notebook

You have already begun to note down your responses to other literature. Now you need the essential piece of equipment which no writer would be caught without. A notebook should be fairly small, because it will be on your person most of the time. I keep mine in the top slot of my rucksack when on holiday, and in my handbag daily. It should always be within easy reach – not in a locked desk or the suitcase which disappeared into the baggage hold!

Hardbacked A5 or A6 sizes are probably the most useful, since these sizes fit most pockets. If necessary, give it a plastic jacket from a specialist stationer or put waterproof tape around the corners, because it helps if your notebook is rain, beverage, and mud-resistant. Cheap notebooks are fine, since whatever you choose will be receiving a battering over the coming months. However, avoid spiral bound books; these fall apart quickly. Choose stapled, stitched, or perfect-bound (flat square-ended spines) wherever possible. Above all, you must want to write in it. Therefore, if you can't face being seen with anything other than rare papers bound in leather, and the thought of keeping your ideas in something worth 50p makes you ill, go right ahead with something special.

Before you start to specialise and find your feet as a writer, it is likely that your range of subject matter is still unknown and unformed. At this stage, your subject matter should be a combination of what's inside you and what's out there – for the simple reason that 'out there' is the place where literature starts and where most of your ideas are destined to arise.

As a beginner, you might not know what to write down, so here are some suggestions:

> ➢ Amusing and poignant comments made by children or the elderly.
> ➢ Snippets of conversation overheard in cafes and other public places.
> ➢ Personal names which suit their jobs: 'Mr Birch, Tree Surgeon'.

> ➢ Gobbledygook from official forms and instruction manuals.
> ➢ Characters and their habits.
> ➢ Put-downs and one-liners which you find particularly good.
> ➢ Incongruous shop names: 'Kurl up n' Dye, Hairdressers'.
> ➢ Your opinions of the environment.
> ➢ Spontaneous rant and criticism.
> ➢ Detailed description of a special item which interests you.

All these suggestions involve you in language and the different forms it takes.

The notebook should preferably focus on what you see, hear, and observe – because that way, it will become more useful to you later on. Such material as that described above can supply you with starting points for poems, missing lines in half-finished works, dramatic lines for your characters, and even whole paragraphs for stories. The next time you are sitting on a train and you see another passenger dive for a notebook even though nothing is happening ... that person is probably a fellow writer.

The Diary

If you're already keeping a daily or weekly account of your life, congratulations. If you keep a diary, it may some day keep you in return, as the poet W.H. Auden once declared. Whether you're an intimate diarist examining yourself and your relationships in detail, or more of a brief 'did this, went there' note-taker, your reactions and observations will help to make you a fluent writer. Looking back on your diary, you might see favourite words and verbal tics appearing repeatedly – noticing such recurrences will help you to avoid them in your creative work.

If you are a poet, you might find that some sentences can be lifted directly for your work, because they contain a good image or an unexpected insight. And the regularity of diary writing will get you used to the situation which all professional writers have to face: that of sitting down at regular times to commit work to paper. Believe it or not, some creative people find this difficult!

If you don't have a personal journal or you find it impossible to keep diaries private, collecting a miscellany or scrapbook will be a good alternative. Some writers keep all three.

The Miscellany or Commonplace Book

The miscellany has a long history. In the remote past, households often kept 'commonplace books' including instructions, notable events, recipes, and national news. A writer's miscellany is much the same. Paste in magazine and newspaper cuttings such as these:

- ➢ Extraordinary human interest stories.
- ➢ Crime cases.
- ➢ Unusual hobbies.
- ➢ Unintentionally comic advertisements.
- ➢ Affecting pieces of journalism.
- ➢ Snippets from interviews with authors and other people that you admire.
- ➢ Intriguing book reviews.
- ➢ Postcards and photographs.

You'll be collecting source material similar to that written in your notebook, except the origins are one step further away from you – it is life observed and recorded by others. It will enable you to find good subjects which you might not think of yourself. Many crime novelists have begun with famous cases excavated from historic newspapers. If you attend any creative writing classes in the future, the tutor may use photographs and other pictures as a starting point; you can do this for yourself by collecting significant images, and asking friends to send you offbeat, artistic, or vintage-style postcards.

Some writers also find the following useful:

Recording Dreams

Keep another notebook near your bed, and write down any significant dream plots or images as soon as you wake. Don't worry if it looks incoherent – as with all notebook jottings, get the material down first, and worry about it later. Many a midnight scrawl has resulted in the genesis of a good poem image; and as a beginner you need as much material as you can collect.

While using whole slabs of your dream diary will strike other readers as self-indulgent, it's a great way of collecting fresh and bizarre images which your conscious everyday mind is automatically screening out. It could be valuable if you intend writing fantasy or horror, or working with visual artists in those genres.

Keeping a dream diary may also help you address issues relating to personal confidence and current bugbears. Over a period of time you may notice recurring images and themes which connect in an associative way to real-life problems.

Start Them Today!

If you haven't got a writers' notebook, commonplace book, diary or journal of any description, start at least one of these today. Attach a pencil on a string to the book, if it seems you never have writing utensils to hand when you need them. I keep a night notebook with a pen tethered to the handle of a drawer – it saves scrabbling about in the dark, because all I have to do is follow the string. I can't make the excuse of 'I couldn't find my notebook' when a good idea strikes me at 2 a.m.

Why should you do any of this, if you already know what you want to write? And if you don't know what to write, why bother with notebooks and diaries first? Here's why:

- ➢ Because you need the practice if you're right at the start.
- ➢ Because you must learn to recognise good subject matter, and this takes time and experience.
- ➢ Because writing has to be part of your everyday life if you want to succeed.
- ➢ Because fun, entertainment, and random ideas will help – you don't want to be a dull writer, do you?

> ➢ Because worries, problems, and obsessions often make powerful subjects.
> ➢ Because when your first good ideas have been used up, you need some more.
> ➢ Because when family and work pressures cut down on your writing time, you need pre-existing material.
> ➢ Because if you enjoy some early success, people might ask you for stories and poems or articles at short notice.

Now that you're keeping a set of notebooks and making entries as often as you can, you can start to think of yourself as a writer.

Thinking like a Writer

What makes writers different from ordinary folk? True, some are driven personalities and others have exceptional talent, but most working writers are people like you who've decided to become good at something. Here are some additional reasons why people write:

> ➢ They read a novel and realise 'I can do better than that'.
> ➢ They are dissatisfied with the available books on their favourite subjects.
> ➢ Styles in contemporary poetry or drama leave them cold.
> ➢ Something traumatic has happened and it helps them psychologically to write about the experience.
> ➢ They want to investigate their family history/local environment.
> ➢ They keep thinking up unusual or unrelated sentences and they just can't help it.

One of those reasons might resonate with you.

Leaving aside any glamour or personality concerns – which are always exaggerated by the media – thinking like a writer often comes down to one main factor. Creative writers tend to see the world around them as subject matter. Nothing is sacred – terrible childhoods, weird neighbours, marital problems, embarrassing incidents – it's all grist to the mill. But if you plan on becoming published, using real life can come with its own dangers. These are primarily the ones of alienating your friends, or causing unexpected dilemmas.

Here is one *faux pas* which happened to me several years ago:

As a result of working in a fraught office with competitive associates, I wrote a satirical poem which was later selected to appear in an anthology. Unknown to me, another two poets from the same town had work destined to appear in the same anthology. One of these had a parent who – yes, you've guessed it – worked in the same building as me. Since they were close, it was inevitable that the parent would see the anthology, thereby exposing my work to the only person in the universe who could recognise the subjects.

The likelihood of this occurring – thousands of poets, national anthology – is so small that it seems impossible, yet it happened. I'm just lucky that I found out in time, through talking to a friend. I rang the publisher, explained my dilemma, and forwarded an altered version of the poem giving fictitious names and titles. This put me in the clear, while the poem itself was still satirical. You can save yourself a lot of hassle by making sure that your real-life subjects are sufficiently disguised – for any public viewing eventuality – at the outset!

When reforming such material into literature, the golden rules should always be:

a) change the names, silly; and
b) alter things enough so that their basis in real-life events aren't so obvious;
c) seek permission if you are writing true-life material about someone you know.

You may be writing a fictitious story, but 'inserted' subjects who recognise themselves or their lives will more than likely be very upset. If publication happens, subjects might resort to legal action if they feel their lives or reputations have been damaged. So disguise is essential even at minor levels.

I'm assured by other writers' tales that 'nobody ever recognises themselves in a book'. But you don't want any more problems than you can handle – keeping going as a writer is complicated enough. You should put all your energy into the story you are telling.

Starting Close to Home

You have to start somewhere, and looking at your own life and background, your relatives and associates, will provide useful leads. If you or your parents have lived abroad, someone has led an unusual life or done things which they shouldn't have done, you struggled to bring up a child on your own, or you meet many different characters in your employment …

… it's all **potential subject matter**. Because what is ordinary and accepted to you may be exotic, interesting, and unusual to a reader. It will be helpful at this point to compile a list of all that you could potentially use, drawn from the following areas:

> ➢ Home life and background (characters, situations).
> ➢ Working life (job details, premises, relationships, customers and clients).
> ➢ Places you visit regularly (clubs, societies, holiday destinations).

Do it now! It won't take too long.

As yet another sheet joins the others in your files, you now have enough prompt material to back up your spontaneous work and any ideas you may already be working on.

If you are restricted to a few hours per week, looking over your lists will generate something before you start to fear the blank page. Perhaps an item on your most recent list connects with an idea or comment written in your notebook? If so, you may have other sentences and ideas which relate to them. This is how creative work often begins.

What Else?

Apart from a willingness to see subject matter everywhere, it also helps if you are open-minded. As a new writer, you could be missing good ideas through making yourself write what you think you ought to write, what seems to be 'nice' or 'acceptable' instead of that gutsy, dark-toned piece which really excites your imagination.

Inspiration

Being open-minded about inspiration may also help. Some writing tutors refuse to believe in this phenomenon, but I've seen class members suddenly leap for their pens as a strong idea strikes them out of nowhere. Regular practice doesn't just encourage words – it enables the real magical thing to happen. What's good enough for Shelley and Shakespeare is good enough for the rest of us; and, as the composer Tchaikovsky once maintained, 'Inspiration is a guest who is reluctant to visit the lazy'.

Emotion

Until you have everything in balance – your styles, plans, ideas, and techniques – write what you think and feel, and not what you think other people want to hear. Forget about publication or performance right now: concentrate on the writing part! Later, when your work has greater craftsmanship and control, you can rework the raw energy and excitement found in your early pieces. To this end: don't over-criticize yourself at first, don't worry about how uncontrolled or emotional it is, and don't throw anything away.

Save your Drafts

You might need a box or lever-arch file to save all your early pieces, and it's important to keep them. For poets, whose work tends to improve in fits and starts, a terrible early poem could contain the seeds of a good one which you only recognise later on. The same thing can happen with unworkable stories containing one excellent character who demands to be excavated and given a decent platform. I regret having thrown away early poem drafts because they were poor or embarrassing. Don't make the same mistake!

Putting the Hours In

Finding the time is a big concern for student writers, but don't let worries about real life and employment put you off. Most established authors began the same way as you, writing their first works in addition to a paid career doing something entirely different. Even quite famous authors can earn very little from their book sales, so a reliable day job is essential. Don't be tempted to 'give up the day job' until you can earn almost the same amount or more from your writing.

Persistence is the key. It's no good writing frantically for ten hours and then doing nothing for two months. One hour a day is sufficient: and, like trying to start a rusty old machine, things will become easier with practice. If you haven't got a theme or a work in progress which you can return to each day, use the hour for diary entries or (for example) a letter to an imaginary person. Get it off your chest; scribble, scrawl, describe the view through the window, put down the first thing you think of and keep going.

> ➢ Try to set aside a regular time each day.
> ➢ Always have a second pen or pencil nearby.
> ➢ Recognise distraction for what it is – resist the temptation to reorganise the wardrobe when you know you should be writing.
> ➢ Hang in there; it takes a while for trees to fruit.

An hour a day may not sound like much, but you will be surprised at the amount you've written after a month. The early 20th century novelist TF Powys was a late starter who managed less than 500 words per day, yet he still wrote several books. If you determine to write a certain amount each day (I have worked aiming for three pages) you are on the way to achieving something. In my case, it was a rough draft for a short novel after three months.

If you are sure that your talent is worth concentrating on, and it becomes necessary to spend more time at it, you may find that your employer will agree to alternative working patterns. The trend towards part-timing and shift work is ideal for new novelists who might otherwise be restricted to a few hours at the weekend.

Finally: a word of warning to writers who want to share their works with their nearest and dearest straight away. Make sure they want to hear about it first. All over the country, living rooms freeze as someone insists on reciting yet another lengthy installment. And then the writer wonders why nobody takes them seriously. Try not to use friends and family as a captive audience; instead, ask for their involvement as plot-suggesters and word-changers when you're stuck. It helps to have people on your side.

Do I Need a Study?

The size needed for your personal writing space will depend on your concentration levels. Consider these points:

> ➤ Are you good at ignoring noise?
> ➤ How important is privacy to you?

If your answers to the above are 'No' and 'Very', writing in the same living space as other people will prove tough.

Singleton writers are often fortunate in this respect, since interruptions can be controlled easily and their space is their own. Yet it's not always necessary to have a personal 'den' – and it's saddening to come across a fully equipped den inhabitant who hasn't a hope of ever writing a decent work!

A lockable drawer and access to a computer, plus the all-important hour or more for writing, are all you need at the start. You don't need a big desk; poems can be achieved just as effectively by sitting on the floor with a clipboard to write on. Many home-based writers use the kitchen table – handy in that it's near the kettle and food supply too. Some prefer a general level of background noise, while others need absolute silence before they can concentrate. Those wooden garden sheds are a useful choice if you must have separate premises and office furniture. Most adolescent writers begin their careers upstairs, writing in the bedroom. The thing to remember is that writing is an adaptable art, and what suits one person won't suit another – pity the visual artist, who needs a studio and lots of clumsy equipment.

Your First Practice Poem

We'll get onto some differences in poetry and prose later, but right now it's time for you to consolidate the note-taking practice you've had during the preceding pages. You're about to produce a poem under guidance, becoming used to poetic imagery and how to use it. To write an effective poem, it helps to remember the following:

> ➢ Poetry and poetic images often have more than one meaning at once. They don't have to make literal sense in the same way as straightforward prose.

Thinking as a poet has lots to do with surprise, and looking at the world with 'a sort of mental squint', as Lewis Carroll once wrote. Your imagination has to be ready to seize opportunities, and it doesn't matter if these are brief and fleeting. Let's practise. For instance, think about dropping a mirror onto the kitchen floor. What images, what sentences spring to mind as you picture that mirror actually hitting the tiles? List them. Here are three, although I'm sure you can manage plenty more:

Ice splinters, bits of sky being reflected;
The end of an illusion;
Superstition about seven years of bad luck.

All of these could be used as the basis for a poem, and such notations are exactly how some poets begin writing one.

As an alternative to listing your ideas, you could try a 'spider diagram'. Place the main subject (a broken mirror) within a circle on the centre of your page, and give this circle outwards-facing 'spokes' like wheel struts. At the end of each spoke write your ideas relating to the central subject. Do this now – it'll give you the skeleton of a real poem, containing ideas unique to you. When writing the poem, you work around the 'wheel' turning each idea into a new line. Put this diagram away for now, and return to it after you've completed the next piece of writing.

When using imagery, there's no set rule on how much you should put in. You can have hardly any images – you might be writing a narrative or conversational poem – or you could have more than one image per line, like this convoluted example from Gerard Manley Hopkins: 'Our hearts' charity's hearth's fire, our thoughts' chivalry's throng's Lord' (from *The Wreck of the Deutschland*, written c.1876).

Here's an example of an image-dense poem which is also well controlled, compact enough not to lose the message, and not at all confusing once the central 'conceit' is understood. Read and think about this poem for about fifteen minutes before continuing.

Prayer

Prayer the Churches banquet, Angels age,
Gods breath in man returning to his birth,
The soul in paraphrase, heart in pilgrimage,
The Christian plummet sounding heaven and earth;
Engine against th'Almightie, sinners towre,
Reversed thunder, Christ-side-piercing spear,
The six-daies world transposing in an houre,
A kind of tune, which all things heare and fear;
Softnesse, and peace, and joy, and love, and blisse,
Exalted Manna, gladnesse of the best,
Heaven in ordinarie, man well drest,
The milkie way, the bird of Paradise,
Church-bels beyond the starres heard, the souls bloud,
The land of spices; something understood.

(George Herbert, c.1630-1633)

plummet: plumb bob, depth measurer
towre: tower

Although some of the individual lines may be hard to follow at first, it's soon apparent what George Herbert is doing in this poem. All the phrases – 'reversed thunder', 'man well drest' – are being used as new descriptions for the traditional idea of prayer. These range from quite homely comparisons (a man in good clothing, a kind of tune) to more abstract, difficult ideas like prayer being a solid refuge or an advantage point like a stone tower.

George Herbert is very economical with his words. He doesn't waste time with padding; he usually has one or two images per line, each of which provides another perspective on his subject. Although he is using a rhyme scheme (in this case, a sonnet – 14 lines) the construction of this poem is basically a list of comparisons, 'how many ways can you describe prayer'. He also has the real poet's gift of making things new. Before this piece, it is unlikely that many people thought of prayer as useful like a good suit of clothes, or like thunder travelling backwards.

So although George Herbert is remote from us in time, and many readers may not identify with the ideas and sentiments he expresses, such a poem makes a good model for achieving something similarly concise, image-based, and fresh.

Your Turn Now

On a new page, write down some abstract qualities, emotions, or states of mind. Suitable ideas would be: anger, hope, disappointment, love. Try to choose something strong and worth writing about! Next, choose one of your suggestions – the one with the greatest number of associations for you – and list as many images or comparisons as you can. Not full sentences or descriptions; aim at brief versions, like George Herbert did.

Try to write at least fifteen images. It may take a long time, and perhaps you will need to return to your page at various points during the day. Don't worry about this; it may even take several attempts over a number of days. Or you may be one of those lucky people who can think up tons of stuff within ten minutes.

Study Tip

If you lose the thread easily, start again by putting your subject at the start of a line, for example 'Anger is like ...' and follow with an image. Then cross out your 'anger is like ...' format, and you will be left with the images you need.

Some of your ideas will sound more like the subject than others, and you may need to return later in the day before seeing which images still work. Select the best ones and form these into an unrhymed poem of at least five lines. Use George Herbert to help you along; sometimes he varies his lines, contrasting one idea per line with two or more in the next. If you are already a verse writer, you might find it possible to fit rhyming endings in – although it may not improve the overall poem! Always use your strongest and most unusual images, not merely what fits the rhyme scheme.

Whether it took you half an hour or several evenings, well done. You have just experienced what it feels like to write an original poem. You may have been frustrated – maybe the lines didn't fit, you couldn't think of what to put, and there's no impressive finish. This happens often in the lives of regular poets, and it can be just the same for prose writers. 'A poem is never finished, it is only abandoned', said the French poet Verlaine.

On your next writing session, take out the previous sheet which you began with the image of a broken mirror, and see if you can complete another poem.

What Is a First Draft?

Whilst reading this handbook you'll notice me mentioning 'drafts' or 'notes'. These are the two raw components which form your written literature. Some people write hurried notes first, complete with abbreviations, different coloured inks, pencil, and a variety of unusual notepapers including paper bags and envelope backs. Others take a tidier approach and form a reasonably complete first draft on sequential sheets of paper; or they might move on quickly from their brief notes to a tidier draft, which then stands as the first base for their work. Some don't bother with paper – everything goes straight onto screen, with the earlier versions being saved to disk.

Whether you're a compact sort of writer or one who is intent on wasting as much spare paper as possible, it's all acceptable as a working method. Just remember which order your random sheets are in, and clarify any unreadable passages before you finish. The latter is important if you can't write every day. It's amazing what you can forget after a week.

Conclusions

Hopefully you have followed all the suggestions I've made in this chapter. Skipping over large sections won't help, as this handbook is cumulative and you might miss something which solves a problem later on. By now you should have:

> ➢ A combination of a notebook and diary/cuttings book in which you are writing daily.
> ➢ The ability to read other literature critically.
> ➢ Fewer worries about making mistakes.
> ➢ An assorted number of ideas and starting points.
> ➢ The ability to find subject matter in the world around you.
> ➢ A completed first poem.

Keep up your notebooks and diaries from now on, because you're going to need them! Besides, I can't tell you what to write beyond a few practise exercises; the ones in this manual are designed to be one-size-fits-all. Your actual subject matter is entirely up to you.

Tutorial Section

Points for Discussion

1. Is there such a thing as originality in writing?
2. Some critics believe that you need special 'poetic' language when you write a poem, while others say that ordinary language is perfectly all right. Which side are you on?
3. Why are diaries still written by people who are not looking to write as a career?
4. Have you an annotated family bible or any old written documents in the attic? What does this documentation tell you about your past or the lives of the people concerned?

Practice Questions

1. You might have seen magnetic fridge poetry sets in bookshops and gift stores. … but you can easily create your own. You will need: several sheets of white A4, your computer or a typewriter, and access to a laminator. Write lists of the words you like, setting them evenly spaced on the paper. Don't forget a few connectors like: 'and', 'or', 'but', 'of'; sprinkle in a few 'a's and 'the's', so that your poetic words will form recognisable phrases. Laminate the paper, and cut the words so that each one is a separate laminated square. Find a small purse or box for your set. Poetry sets like these are ideal for using on lap trays and coffee tables, or you could buy a pack of magnets from a craft shop and convert your words for use on a fridge.
2. Where else can you derive subject matter? Not all possibilities are explored in this chapter.
3. Compile a time line (either horizontal or vertical) and place significant dates or years on one side of the line, with a sentence or two on what was happening in the wider world. On the other side, write corresponding significant incidents from your life. Now interview a relative or close friend, and compile a personal time line for them. Recording accurately dated incidents is a useful skill for biographers and local historians, who often compile time lines as a first step when organising their material.

2 Practical Stuff

One Minute Overview

You're on the road as a new writer, yet you know that your grammar and spelling isn't all it should be. Or, the spelling part is fine, but you have no idea about where to find information on the current writing scene, and how many people publish the type of work you want to write. You might have good ideas but no structure in mind, or you don't know your dizaine from a dodo. Fear not, for help is at hand. This chapter will outline some of the basics you should know if you want your writing to improve. There's no excuse for weak lines or hopeless grammar – it really isn't as difficult as you thought.

Essential Reference Kit

Handbook / Yearbook

No writer should be without one of the following: *The Writer's and Artist's Yearbook* (A & C Black, yearly) or *The Writer's Handbook* (ed. Barry Turner, Macmillan, yearly). You'll obtain the same brilliant information from either – it's just a matter of taste. I favour the *Handbook* because the typeface is a bit more reader-friendly, the layout is less cramped, and it tends to be more up-front about publishers' requirements and the royalty system. But the *Yearbook* will get you there just the same, and it's more useful if you work with visual arts.

However, these books are being compiled the year before they appear; the details for this year will have been finalised in last year, and so on. This can create issues. Staff may have moved on, agents change their names, small presses may have become dormant, big publishers may have takeovers. It's as well to remember this. So before you post off a speculative book proposal or your first three chapters, check that the publisher is still there. A brief email or phone call to the main switchboard will save you a lot of wasted time and postage expense.

The *Yearbook/Handbook* is nevertheless packed with relevant addresses and chapters of advice from professional writers, including those from the TV and media world. Separate editions are available for children's writers and internet-based literature; these are published by A & C Black on the same rolling programme as the *Yearbook*. They form some of the most reliable reference books you are likely to need. But they aren't very cheap. If it feels like money down the pan at your current stage of development, you can find copies of this and the *Yearbook* in the reference section of your public library.

While not wanting to be a free publicist for either of those books, you really can't go wrong; they provide arts council addresses, prizes, bursary and festival information, and literary clubs of all descriptions. In fact, they have everything you'll need once you are experienced enough to think about publication. They will save you time too, particularly if you are working without the help of a writing class or similar network.

Dictionary

Go on, treat yourself to one. Not a miniscule palm-sized one, but a stonking great doorstep of over 68,000 entries, from Collins, Penguin, or any of the other literary publishers. A substantial one will have more than just extra words – contexts and correct usage will also be provided, along with sample proverbs and word origins. Some old-fashioned editions have an appendix with common Latin phrases and arcane abbreviations too – good reference material if you're writing stuffy characters with letters after their names.

People without much knowledge of grammatical points (like: the various parts of a sentence) will find it all in a dictionary, where each entry is followed by its type – n (noun) adj. (adjective) pr. (pronoun). Then look up 'adjective' and 'pronoun' to find out what they are and how they're used …

before you know it, your dictionary will become a treasury of information rather than a forbidding-looking item on the shelf.

Thesaurus

One of these, or a dictionary of synonyms and antonyms, will help you to find the right words when you're stuck. Can't think of a suitable alternative to a word you've just used in the last sentence? Look it up in a thesaurus, and the equivalents are provided. Books of synonyms (similar words) and antonyms (opposite words) achieve the same ends, and some publishers provide antonyms in a combined volume with a thesaurus. Roget's Thesaurus is the well-known brand, but there are others. Having one of these will give you plenty of word power, but over-use might make you sound stilted and pedantic. Sometimes, an 'equivalent' word just doesn't have the same associations as the right word.

Rhyming Dictionary

This is indispensable for new poets, because a good one can provide a whole introduction to the art form. Frances Stillman's *The Poet's Manual and Rhyming Dictionary* is a popular choice, and although I have one with a typeface which makes everything harder and duller than it should be, it has all the information I'm likely to need if I write rhyming verse. Apart from one, two, and three syllable rhymes, it provides explanations and examples of every common scheme from couplet to sonnet and sestina, through ancient lesser-used forms like the rondel and ballade royale. If a poet has used it, it's probably in here.

We'll be looking at a few popular rhyme schemes later on, but some people absolutely love complicated rhyming and the 'beginner' forms described by me are not challenging enough. If this is you, try the examples in Stillman.

Historical Reference

You might think this only applies to those who are writing period sagas. But you never know when a fact or a date may need checking – one of your characters might refer to an event they witnessed, or you might write a poem based on life in Ancient Egypt. You could have a fictional examinee trying to pass a test, and you don't know the answer they have to supply.

Unless you're already an expert in the area, a selection of reference books will prevent re-writes and plots that can't work because the dates are wrong. I have a pocket guide to British History, which lists kings and queens, major historical events, inventions, and discoveries. It's all I need to prevent my heroine in 1902 from referring to Queen Victoria, when it's King Edward on the throne. And she won't be driving around in a Rolls Royce, because they haven't been invented just yet. A few reference works will save you an awful lot of time, yet they can be picked up for next to nothing at discount bookstores.

Your Public Library

Despite being run down over the past two decades, the public library service is still magnificent and ... under-used. Apart from having all the reference books you need, you can check the literary periodicals such as *The Bookseller* and the *Times Literary Supplement*; they may have details about local writers' events or a leaflet rack supplying competitions forms. And you automatically have access to the interlibrary loan service, which operates within your county and throughout the UK. Yes! If they haven't got the book on their premises, you can have it sent. Sometimes it can be there within three days. Cost? Pennies. That's better than mail-order. Thus, your average shoebox-sized branch library has the interior dimensions of a Tardis. What a magical place it is.

The Tardis is the space ship used by the Doctor in the BBC series Dr Who

Research

Perhaps you are historically inclined and basic reference material isn't enough; you have ideas for serious literature set in the past, or a piece that needs detailed research, and you don't want a mere passable impression created by a few strategically-placed references. If you live near a university with a notable library, it's worth enquiring there for an external reader's ticket. But don't ignore the public library – some of the city ones have amazing resources, and special collections donated by benefactors. For instance: Birmingham Central Library has a First World War poets' collection which is comparable to that in the university. Reference sections will have other useful things like:

Newspapers on microfilm or similar
Who's Who and *Who Was Who*
Brewer's *Dictionary of Phrase and Fable*
Bartlett's *Quotations*/the *Oxford Dictionary of Quotations*
Legal statutes and law books
Local history, parish maps, and architectural information.

For serious researchers, it's possible to join the British Library. They have literally miles of books, stored under the streets of London and accessible with a plastic ticket and some form of identification. If you're writing as a casual hobby, you don't need the British Library – but I'd recommend it to anyone who's engaged on a book needing more than your imagination. Specialised non-fiction writers, biographers and historical fictioneers would benefit from a ticket. When researching:

> Don't read aimlessly – have some idea of what you want to discover and record beforehand.
> Turn to the book index first – what you want may be listed clearly there.
> Take notes; facts, incidents, and attributed opinions are probably what you need, not whole pages. Reduce what you see, and put it in your own words where possible – as opposed to copying out whole paragraphs exactly.
> Use pencils – archive libraries don't allow pens.

I hope all this has given you the confidence to explore the libraries near you. Some of these sections are proving a bit dry, and there's worse to come. Yet starters need reliable information, not any old stuff – which leads me neatly on to the next point.

Computers and the Internet

Yes, the Internet is a valuable resource, characterised by freedom, democracy and access. You might not even have to leave your house to make your discoveries. But the sheer number of sites is more likely to increase your research time than cut it down. Websites are set up by anyone, often maintained by nobody. There are many sites on aspects of literature and writing, with conflicting dates, omissions, links that refuse to work, unchecked spellings, and out-of-date information.

There are even reviews of books that don't exist, written by people under assumed names; and hatchet-jobs written by literary rivals with a grudge. As it's all happening in cyberspace, there's no way of knowing what's real. You don't want any of that to appear in your articles. Researching by the internet alone is very much a shot in the dark – try to back up your information with real books written by qualified people.

The computer – how could I have failed to mention it earlier? You can load up with all kinds of software which will almost write the book for you, and there's an on-board thesaurus and spellchecker too. These functions are handy, but don't forget that the computer is a machine. It can't really understand what you're writing, and it probably speaks American. Therefore, the context of your words can't be judged, and it will miss some spellings. Place-names or character names might be silently altered by the 'intuitive' program, and you only discover this after having printed out fifty pages. How annoying.

While computers enhance and present your work, they're not the ones with the talent. You are the power-unit which needs development. A notebook and pen won't crash or develop a virus, and they're far more use should you have that great idea while sitting in the park. That's why I'm placing more emphasis on the low-tech aspects of writing. Creativity comes from human beings, and it's that human contact which makes it special. Moreover, if you're not prepared to use your mind and talents, no amount of expensive software will turn you into a writer.

> **Study Tip**
> Don't spoil your creativity and narrative flow by looking up every single thing you're not sure about. Write it first, check it afterwards. Leave blanks if you can't find the date or the name. Also leave blanks if you don't have the exact brand name for a product or the right surname for a character. Crack on with your script while the ideas are fresh and you're motivated.

Improving Your Punctuation and Grammar

Thanks to the phenomenal sales of Lynne Truss' book *Eats, Shoots, and Leaves*, grammar and punctuation are back on the agenda. Many of us were not taught these subjects successfully at school – it was something we caught onto, if lucky, by accident. While learning French verbs, it never occurred to me that English did that too; that the verb 'to be' was so irregular that it changes from 'I *am*' to 'you *are*' and he/she *is*' instead of doing the sensible thing and remaining as 'be'. You don't need grammatical perfection to become a good writer; not in the first draft anyway. But it helps if you can avoid the silly mistakes which scream 'amateur' and 'inept' to the first writing tutor or editor who sees your work.

It may sound geeky and annoying, but these things matter to editors, script-readers, and anyone else who assesses your work. For example: writers who don't use paragraphs will find their work rejected without delay, because it indicates someone who doesn't know enough about writing.

Start improving your writing now. If you are hazy about what you were told at school, a verb is a **doing** word, and a noun is a **naming** word. Adjectives and adverbs often end in '-ly' and they are used to modify what was previously written. A straightforward sentence has a subject (I) and a verb (go) followed by an object (to the cinema). And sentences are made up of **clauses**, which are units of sense separated by your punctuation. Now commit the following lines to memory, and overcome some of the basic no-no's which bedevil scripts from the English speaking world.

> Over-using the ! will give your writing an hysterical tone.

> Too many clauses in (parentheses) are confusing. They will make the reader lose the plot.

> Sentences which are far too long will sound garbled and uncontrolled – look at how many changes of direction happen within the sentence, and break it up accordingly.

> Lazy writing, such as using 'get' as a substitute for many verbs and actions, will seriously impair the artistic value of your work.

> The problem with 'it' – writers in a hurry often forget to define what 'it' actually is. There shouldn't be any doubt about what 'it' refers to.

> Don't confuse 'their', 'they're', and 'there'. Younger writers who are more used to audiovisual information will often mix these up.

Their is **belonging** and **possession** – their coats.
They're is a **contraction** for 'they are'.
There is **placement** – over there. Also used as a grammatical addition for the verb 'to be' – there is, there are, there were.

> Younger writers tend to run words together: 'alot' being a favourite. Unless accepted as a compound construction in a dictionary, this is simply wrong.

> 'Could of' and 'should of' are also wrong. It's 'could have' and 'should have'.

Down to the Detail

> Avoid greengrocer's apostrophe – potatoe's, carrot's. It's potatoes and carrots. Apostrophes should indicate elision or possession – not plural.
More apostrophe trouble:

Writer's means belonging to a single writer: the writer's pen.
Writers' means belonging to more than one writer: the writers' pens.

It's means 'it is' or 'it has'.

Its indicates belonging – the hound licked its coat.

➢ 'I before e except after c' in most cases – remember about receipt, ceiling, and seize – three of the most common spellings you are likely to meet in this form.

➢ Colons (:) come before a list: carrots, potatoes, leeks, and swede.

➢ List items are always separated by commas, like in the previous line.

➢ Semi colons (;) are useful to point out two contrasting phrases; but over-use can sound stuffy and old-fashioned.

➢ Missing pronouns (I, you, he/she, it, we, they) are clumsy. Readers might miss who you mean when you've written a long sentence involving more than one person.

➢ The split infinitive is regarded as wrong. This is where a whole verb (to see, to do) is disrupted by a modifying word. The famous example is 'to boldly go' from the Star Trek series. The correct form is 'to go boldly' – even though it doesn't sound quite so forceful!

➢ Too many American words – 'gotten', 'parking lot', 'station wagon', 'autopsy', 'gas station', 'elevator' (meaning 'lift') – appear in British English texts. We have town centres, not 'malls'. Transatlantic mannerisms are hard to avoid – there's even some in this book. Just don't let them dominate your writing.

➢ The same goes for unconscious Australianisms: 'barbies', 'tinnies', 'utes'. If you're not writing an Aussie character, kick the tinnies out.

Adjectives, Adverbs, and Modifiers

Now this is a big one. Writing tutors always recommend that too many modifiers and anything ending in '-ly' should be used with caution. Modifying words like 'quite', 'perhaps', and 'probably' will make your sentences sound weaker and less sure of themselves; compare 'the room was quite large' with 'the room was large'. They don't mean the same thing.

Poems thick with adjectives sound fussy and amateur, while a writer who insists on modifying every line of speech with 'loudly', 'strongly' 'sadly' 'emotionally' etc. is heading for the paper-bin. Editors find this annoying because the speech itself should suggest the manner in which it's read, for example:

'Get off my foot!' he yelled. Not: 'Get off my foot!' he yelled loudly and painfully.

We understand that the person is speaking loudly because he is yelling, and there is an exclamation mark to indicate surprise and a raised tone of voice. So 'loudly' in this case is redundant. If you check back on your scripts and throw out a few of these redundant words, a clogged script might read fluent and lively instead. It makes a more fluent transition to the next potential line if 'painfully' is also cut out of the sample sentence above.

Active and Passive

When writing, try to use the **active** voice rather than the **passive**. By this, writing tutors mean that you should avoid using an impersonal tone of voice, which doesn't clearly indicate who is doing what, and which is more suited to business reports and official forms.

'it is often thought that ...' instead of 'we often think' and

'the sandwich was picked up by James' instead of 'James picked up the sandwich'

are two examples of a passive voice being replaced by an active one. Too much passive voice in your work will kill it off. It's a danger you may fall into if your everyday work involves officialese and staying professionally detached. You can see examples of it everywhere – a train timetable on my desk right now states 'in order to consolidate' and 'in order to provide' instead of 'to consolidate' and 'to provide'. This stiff old stuff isn't creative writing.

You can bet that anything in a passive voice will be written by someone covering up for uncertainties and a personality shortage.

More on layout

> Speech marks should enclose anything said by a character. Also use them for quotations taken from another source. If you use double speech marks, stay consistent – don't change to single ones halfway through your story. A few literary stylists will use dashes instead of speech marks, but an editor or reader will find traditional speech marks easier.
> Sentences about the same thing should be bunched together in paragraphs. Paragraphs give the reader a breathing space and allow them to understand your text. Good paragraphing makes all the difference to a complicated or technical episode, and short paragraphs are essential if you are writing journalism or similar articles for a wide readership.

If you can sort your apostrophes and put them in the right places, you will be halfway towards pleasing an editor. You wouldn't believe the number of people who plaster their scripts with the wrong 'it's'/'its'.

Anything Else?

Some of these bad writing traits can be used to your advantage creatively. The character of an excited teenager may well over-use the exclamation mark in speech and writing; while a bracket-stuffed sentence might be exactly what you need to convey the impression of a long-winded vague character. And the passive voice could be used to portray someone with thought disorders. The difference is:

You must be aware of what you're doing, making punctuation, language choice and grammar serve your ends, instead of you remaining oblivious to the effects you are creating.

A trip to WH Smith's will supply you with enough grammar guides to choose from. A plain no-frills school textbook is all you need; it'll have the same facts as more fashionable guides. You do want to write decent English don't you? Not the sort written by ignorant pretenders?

Then get some kit. Look at it this way. If you were learning tennis, it might help if you had the right racquet and ball for the job.

If you're really confused about 'correct' English and you want more guidance in this area, there's a wonderful handbook which tells you everything: it's the *Good English Guide*, by Graham King (Harper Collins, 2003).

> ### Study Tip
> He said, she said ... Prevent too much repetition by having the list of alternatives handy: answered, replied, muttered, etc. If the speakers are obvious to the reader, it may be possible to dispense with all your 'said's and 'answered's for short periods, and it is particularly appropriate when you are wishing to write a short, fast, tension-filled conversation between characters.

Conclusions

You know which reference books will provide detailed guidance once you're writing your own works as opposed to practice exercises and notes.

You can avoid the main grammatical howlers which make your works look poorly written.

Tutorial Section

Points for Discussion

1. Why is correct grammar necessary? After all, plenty of people don't bother with it.
2. Spelling was irregular and phonetic until printed literature became common. Why should we have regulated spelling now?
3. Do you believe that incorrect spellings and grammar are acceptable in 'creative' forms such as poetry?

Practice Questions

1. What grammatical tics or commonly repeated spelling mistakes have you discovered in your work so far? List them. Put the correct forms alongside, and pin this list near to where you normally write. Refer to it in the future.
2. Where are the writers' help manuals located in your nearest library?
3. Explain the differences between these pairs of words:

stationery	affect	through
stationary	effect	thorough

4. Search through some broadsheet newspapers to find examples of sentences written in the passive voice. Why do you think the journalist has written them in this form?

Focusing on Poetry, Prose and Short Stories

One Minute Overview

So now you're more clued up about spelling, grammar and structure in an abstract way, but how do you apply language knowledge to the particular poem or short story you've had in mind? What are the differences between prose and poetry anyway? Or; your rhythm, rhyme and imagery come easy, but worrying about how to drive a plot forward leaves your writing moving at a glacial pace. Then, there's genre. You might have little idea of what it is, never mind which one your work should fit into, if any. Read on and it will all become clear.

Prose or Poetry?

Defining prose and poetry can keep academics occupied for centuries. Samuel Taylor Coleridge thought the following:

> I wish our clever young poets would remember my homely definitions of prose and poetry; that is, prose = words in their best order; poetry = the best words in the best order.

> (quoted in *Topics in Criticism*, ed. Butler & Fowler, Longman, 1978).

But modern novelists would argue they're striving to put the best words in the best order too. And so on. Things have changed since Coleridge's day! Now, there are poetic novelists and poets who write prose poems. You can write experimental prose fragments in non-standard layouts, or describe a hundred-page series of couplets as a novel in verse. Where does it stop, I hear you ask.

Kicking down the boundaries between genres is all very well, but how does this help the new writer? Not much, in the first instance, because you still have to know about genres and styles before knowing which rules to break and discovering how experimental you are. Here are some basic points to help you sort one from the other, building on the definition given in Chapter 1.

Prose is mostly linear – beginnings, middles and ends, conflict and resolve, characters moving from one state to another, timescales happening, stories and narratives. Generally understood on first reading. This book is written in prose, using a set of guidelines including 'educational' and 'plain'. And the following example is a different type of narrative voice with a poetic descriptive tone:

> The stooping figure of my mother, waist deep in the grass and caught there like a piece of sheep's wool, was the last I saw of my country home as I left to discover the world.
>
> As I Walked Out One Midsummer Morning,
> Laurie Lee, (Penguin 1971).

Poetry is mostly associative – a denser use of imagery, less reliance on plot, short bursts as opposed to marathons. Often needs repeat readings before the meaning is clear. Self-contained and elusive. Patterning using rhythm and rhyme.

> There was a young lady from Leeds
> Who swallowed a packet of seeds

and

> In Xanadu did Kubla Khan
> A stately pleasure dome decree

are both examples of poetry: the former being the first two lines of a limerick, the latter being a piece of Samuel Taylor Coleridge's high-flown Romantic manner.

Within these broad definitions there are other genres and styles. Popular genres of prose would include: romance, thriller, science fiction, biography, and journalism. In the past, genres would have included the epistolatory novel (told through letters) and picaresque (bawdy adventures).

In poetry today you might be predominantly a lyric poet, a political poet, a nature poet, a stand-up comedian. Centuries ago you might have been an epic poet, a tragedian or a satirist.

Things move on; can you spot the next trend?

Why Bother with Genre?

Knowing your genres and pathways will greatly help when you are marketing and placing your work. On the whole, publishers can't sell books which fall between genres. Their marketing people aren't geared up for it, and they are governed by financial constraints. Therefore, if you are aiming at publishing and entertaining, it helps if your work fits neatly into one of the already recognised genres.

Experimental works that cross genres are the exceptions which prove the rule. Literary critics praise out-there material, and so do specialised cult readerships; but the mass book-buying public prefers clearer cut divisions and understandable genres. So do bookshop owners, who'll want to know where to put your volume on their shelves.

At the beginning, it doesn't matter – just develop your talent first. You won't know which route to take for a while, and that's why it's so important to have notebooks on the go. You may think that your natural sphere is as a writer of social comedy and you may be seen as a regular unthreatening domestic type at home. But there could be a sci-fi and fantasy prizewinner trying to break out. None of this will be apparent unless you try a few different genres first. And it's better to make mistakes early on in your writing career.

Which Genre is for Me?

If you're writing plenty of assorted pieces but an overall direction hasn't yet appeared, the following exercise may help.

On a new sheet of paper, write a list of the genres and styles you have enjoyed in the past (including any television or film versions of books), noting the particular titles under the appropriate headings. Take some time over it; remember books from childhood, since there may be an overall pattern to your genre choices even though the book was for a child. Next, write a list of genres and types of books you definitely don't like. Now you know where your strengths might lie as a writer, because of the plots and styles which interested you. The knowledge of how such plots work is stacked away in your creative subconscious mind.

But it doesn't end there. Now you have to work out which of your personal characteristics suit which genres. Think about matters like these:

> Are you able to keep on relentlessly with any project for a long time? This is essential for novelists. Being determined is more use to you than 'talent' when a problem occurs.

> Be honest – would you prefer to slob out in front of the soaps on TV rather than plough through an unabridged version of *Wuthering Heights*? Why not write a TV drama?

> Do you lose interest quickly? Butterfly mind? Short forms like poetry may be more suitable.

> Are you very interested in people and what makes them tick, as opposed to images, things and ideas? If so, you will be good at depicting character and motivation – essential for believable stories. But if the reverse is true, poetry may be more natural.

> Good at doing research, but hopeless at plots and imagery? Non-fiction is your best bet. Biographies, ready-made characters, true historical fiction, docudrama; it's a wide field and there's plenty of choice when you think about it.

> Strong visual imagination and/or described as an over-sensitive person? You'll write some terrific poems.

> Think about the time factor – novels may be demoralising if you can only spare odd moments on the train to work.

> ➢ Already experienced in amateur theatre? Then it's
> easier for you to start as a playwright first. Dialogue
> can be rewritten into a novel later on, or reformed as
> monologue poems.

It's handy to establish those types of work you know you definitely won't be any good at – simply because it saves time! Many writers spend years on the wrong stuff, and it's no good forcing yourself to be a playwright when you're really a poet.

> **Study Tip**
> Acknowledging your strengths is more useful than worrying about your shortcomings.

Form in Poetry

Without the following building blocks, whatever you write will probably not look or sound like a poem. Take the time to understand a few things about rhyme and rhythm before embarking on more poems of your own – for while poems are very satisfying to write, it's all too easy to become a wannabe poet who never makes the grade. If you learn some of these traditional basics, you will always know what's wrong when you look at your work in future. Missing beats and ill-contrived imagery will stand out clearly once you know 'what not to wear' as a poet.

Rhythm

Language is made up of rhythmic beats, comprising of stressed and unstressed syllables. A syllable is: part of a word including a vowel or vowel sound. The word in-clu-ding has three. A pattern of syllables arranged in a regular way is called **metre**. English tends to be iambic – one stressed (/) and one unstressed (X) syllable:

X / X / X /
The cat | sat on | the mat.

Here, there are three iambic 'feet', one after the other. Regular successions of these give your work its 'beat' when the lines are arranged into poems. Here's the first line of Thomas Gray's *Elegy on an English Country Churchyard,* which shows the iambic rhythm: 'The curfew tolls the knell of parting day'. Write this line on a separate piece of paper and put in where you envisage the stressed and unstressed syllables to be.

There are other rhythms too: here's a trochee: / X and a dactyl: / X X and an anapaest: X X /. A different mixture of beats will give your poem its rhythmic variety, contributing to speed, intensity, and climax.

Sometimes you won't notice the rhythm while you are writing, particularly if you have a powerful idea driving you along! But beware the following: thumpetty thump, thumpetty thump, thumpetty thump. An unchanging clockwork rhythm will start to dominate your piece, unless you are imitating a specific sound. Many poems about trains successfully depict the rhythm: read WH Auden's famous 'Night Mail' (*Collected Shorter Poems*) for an example.

Other poets deliberately change their rhythm to achieve noticeable effects. In Shelley's 'Ozymandias', a halting heavily stressed rhythm gives way to a regular iambic one on the last line, emphasising the flat landscape leading to eternity: 'the lone and level sands stretch far away'.

Rhyme

Poets who like tradition often start with rhyming verse. It's particularly good for storytelling and comedy, if you're a beginner. The great poems of the past, whether by Chaucer, Shakespeare, or Tennyson, were all by expert rhymers, and a command of different rhyme schemes was essential back then if you wanted to be a poet. But after 1900 'free verse' began to predominate for serious, exploratory subject matter. This is unrhymed, and instead governed by rhythm, image, and syllable counts. DH Lawrence, Robert Frost, and TS Eliot were notable for their experiments in free verse. They're a good place to start if you're pulling away from rhyme and you're interested in literary history.

If you prefer rhyming, a few of the common schemes are set out next. While analysing poetry, critics use a sequence of a, b, c, d ... to work out what rhymes with what, so it's useful if you become used to this method now.

Couplet

A knyght ther was, and that a worthy man   a

That fro the tyme that he first bigan   a

        (from the *Prologue* to Chaucer's *Canterbury Tales*)

A starting couplet like this would be followed by b,b, c,c, d,d ... you'll soon see how it works. Next, we move on to four-lined verses, usually laid out like this:

Quatrain

(1)	or (2)
a	a
b	b
a	b
b	a

or (3)   Mary had a little lamb (unrhymed)

        Its fleece was white as snow(a)

        And everywhere that Mary went (unrhymed)

        The lamb was sure to go. (a)

Quatrains are often called ballad metre, used in folk poetry and traditional song. Method 3 is the easiest, because you only have to find one rhyme for each stanza! Begin with this one, and discover just how flexible it can be. The poet Charles Causley (1917–2003) wrote many ballad-style works. Our second example here was used to amazing effect by Tennyson in his epic poem *In Memoriam*, proving that four-lined stanzas can really go the distance when it comes to important subjects.

Sonnet

You've already met a sonnet by George Herbert in Chapter 1. But there are several distinct types, shown as follows:

(1)   a, b, b, a, a, b, b, a,   c, d, e, c, d, e

        or: c, d, c, d, c, d.

The first version here is called a Petrarchan sonnet, named after the Italian poet Petrarch (1304–1372). It comprises of two parts, the octave (eight lines) and the sestet (six lines). In the first part, a situation is set up; in the second, we have its resolution, answer or reversal. You'll find this pleasantly balanced structure in sonnets from every century.

(2)   a, b, a, b, c, d, c, d, e, f, e, f, g, g.

The second rhyme scheme is a Shakespearian sonnet, popularised but not invented by him; it was another Italian import. It's good for a flexible argument with a sharp or undercutting conclusion on the end couplet.

(3)   a, b, a, b, b, c, b, c, c, d, c, d, e, e.

The third version shown here is a Spenserian sonnet, named after Edmund Spenser (1552 –1599). As it involves fewer rhymes spread over a greater distance, it is difficult to do without sounding artificial. In Spenser's day, sounding ornate and artificial was the whole point. But modern readers might not share that opinion, since lines can appear too contrived and the end rhymes may be too insistent.

Ottava Rima

This was popularised by Lord Byron in *Don Juan*, and it is still occasionally used by poets who want something epic or satirical. As the name implies, it is Italian in origin. It runs:

(first verse) a, b, a, b, a, b, c, c (second verse) d, e, d, e, d, e, f, f (third verse) g, h, g, h, g, h, i, i…..

There's no limit to the number of stanzas you can have on this one. As Byron proves, you can get up a great narrative head of steam with it.

Villanelle

This is an ancient medieval French form (the Troubadors were expert at inventing verses) along with the triolet and rondel. Inexplicably, the villanelle is popular with writing classes and it's worth having one or two up your sleeve. It tends to be fairly short because of the repetitive scheme based on only two rhymes:

a^*, b, a^+ a, b, a^* a, b, a^+ a, b, a^* a, b, a^+ a, b, a^*, a^+

As you can see, a rhyme from one stanza is carried over into the next, and it involves repeating two whole lines more than once (represented here by a^* and a^+). The effect is one of knitting with words, but in the right hands, a villanelle sounds light, polished, and elegant.

Irregular Rhyme

You needn't stick to a rigid scheme of course – many rhyming poems are in irregular verse without a strict pattern to the a's, b's and c's. This has the advantage of being less bound by tradition and expectations, and is more suited to messy contemporary life. Formality and shape can be supplied by dividing your poem into stanza-like blocks, or having roughly the same number of syllables in each line.

Half Rhyme

Used and popularised by Wilfred Owen (1893–1918), although his exact contemporary Ivor Gurney used it, and Emily Dickinson had beaten them to the goalpost before 1880. As implied, this not-quite rhyme depends on a vowel or consonantal chime rather than a full monty: a half rhyme would be 'cot/cat' instead of 'cat/mat'. Here are two lines from Wilfred Owen to show you how it's done:

> It seemed that out of battle I escaped
> Down some profound dull tunnel, long since scooped …
>
> > ('Strange Meeting').

Half-rhyme gives you a wider word choice, but you have to be careful that it doesn't look like a mistake, for example, completing a sonnet and engineering one half-rhyme when everyone can see it should be a full one. Instead of that nicely chiming vowel or consonant, you get a tinny clunk like a cracked bell.

Problems with Rhyme

Recognising some of these in advance (committed by student writers of all ages!) will help you avoid the same in your work.

> ➢ Overdoing it – using one rhyme throughout your poem.
>
> ➢ Breaking form – starting with a quatrain and changing to couplets after a few stanzas.
>
> ➢ Trying rhyme and then giving up, concluding in free verse.
>
> ➢ Using the wrong word with the wrong associations just because it rhymes.
>
> ➢ Remember the point about archaism and word inversions, supplied later.
>
> ➢ Letting your rhyme drive the poem instead of the subject matter.
>
> ➢ Too many clichéd rhymes, like moon/June, love/dove in a love poem.

Writing a few of the above offences will result in a poor poem. It's OK if you're just entertaining yourself or writing a birthday card message, but it's not OK if you plan on submitting your work for readings, anthologies, and competitions. Unfortunately, writers often have no critical judgement over their poems, and they simply can't tell that they've written a stinker! That's why it's important to read poetry and follow the works of at least one contemporary poet. You'll become used to what works and what doesn't.

> **Study Tip**
> Find out more about rhyme by getting a standard anthology – the *Penguin Book of English Verse* or Faber's *The Rattle Bag* (ed. Seamus Heaney and Ted Hughes) and trying out some a,b,c, notations alongside the verses. You'll soon see what the expert poets have done.

Imagery

This is the third leg of our poetry tripod. Without it, your poem falls over because it's flat and two-dimensional. Imagery works equally well in prose, but a large number of images are more appropriate in poems. Ingenious, fresh, and new-minted images are what make a good poem. Deficiencies in other areas can be overcome if you're a stunning writer of images first; so if in doubt, forget about the rhyme and concentrate on making the reader see the picture.

There are two types of images:

Simile – a straightforward comparison using 'like' or 'as'
'My heart is like a singing bird'

(Christina Rossetti)

'Jane, Jane, tall as a crane'

(Edith Sitwell)

and

Metaphor – a trickier direct comparison without the use of 'like' or 'as'

'…and the heron/Priested shore…'

(Dylan Thomas).

In this example, the heron (tall, singular and grey) patrols the shoreline like a priest watching over a congregation. Thomas invents a new verb 'to priest' when describing his unique view of the heron. And this verb is used as an image in place of a simile: 'the heron looks like a priest on the shore' sounds prosaic and far less exciting than the poetic version written by Thomas. Any comparison which makes you think is likely to be a metaphor. Here are a two more, taken from poets often studied at college:

'The shutter of time' (Louis MacNeice)

'Beauty is truth, truth beauty' (John Keats)

Two techniques allied to imagery are: **allusion** and **personification**. In allusion, you might be writing a line which indirectly refers to another branch of literature or life – in reading it, the student will automatically think of the corresponding art form using the clues you have cunningly laid. It gives added depth to a poem. In personification, an item is given prominence by being made to sound like a human character, as in this famous line by Walter de la Mare: 'I spied John Mouldy in his cellar'. Here, wet mould is compared to an old character living down below, his home overrun with rats and dripping water.

Poetry is a world where things have multiple meanings. Trees are like people and people are like trees. One thing often stands for something else. You can have **symbols**, where one image represents something 'big' in your poetic universe, reappearing at significant moments in your poem. And you can use **onomatopoeia**, an unwieldy Greek word that means something quite simple: words which sound like what they represent. Bang! Splat! Woof!

Sometimes you just don't get it, particularly if the poet is an academic or prides himself on being difficult. Never let this put you off. There are plenty of understandable poets out there, writing tomorrow's classics. Explore publishers' lists online to find samples of work you can enjoy.

Problems with Imagery

As implied above, it's all too easy to sound disconnected and hermetically sealed, writing images that don't connect. Common causes are:

- ➤ References to books which nobody except you and your circle have read.
- ➤ Oddball personal symbols which don't communicate, for example, bow ties as the Antichrist, wild flowers as symbols of a materialistic world, mountains as public transport.
- ➤ Mixed and redundant metaphors – when the associations around one half of your image don't fit the associations of the comparison you are using: 'my heart is like a singing doorknob', '… the heron/Cooked the shore …', 'I spied Mrs. Tiggywinkle in the cellar.'

Some experimental poets deliberately use mixed metaphors, and there's no reason why you can't do it. But if you want to communicate, best leave off. Have a look at the different types of images used by poets in the anthologies recommended earlier: *The Rattle Bag* and *The Penguin Book of English Verse*. Contemporary poets can be read in two anthologies published by Bloodaxe Books, *Poetry with an Edge* and *Staying Alive*.

Defining a Short Story

There's a few extra rules needed here. A short story isn't like a shrunk-down novel, although both are in prose. The short story has a structure all of its own, one which must be borne in mind when looking at the outlets available.

Most short stories are destined to appear in women's magazines, with arts-council sponsored anthologies and a few literary journals as a narrower alternative. These outlets have strict word-limits, often as low as one thousand for a one-page magazine slot, three to four thousand, if you're lucky, for the literary journals.

Now you can see the problem. A novel plot, with its multiple characters, several incidents and inter-connected themes, will simply not work under those circumstances. You can't develop a character to any great extent, or spend ages building up an atmosphere of suspense, or let rip with non-stop action sequences. You can't have too many characters crowding in – there isn't the room. Just covering the 'who, what, and where' of your story can use up two hundred of your precious thousand words.

'The end of the world' is probably not a good subject for a short story. Instead, look at one aspect of your overall idea, and redefine the boundaries. Think about:

> ➢ Few characters, one issue, one obstacle or conflict.
> ➢ A limited timespan – one day; one afternoon; three hours.
> ➢ One outcome, realisation, or result.
> ➢ One or two locations.
> ➢ Dive straight in – you can't waste a single word.
> ➢ Every detail should be relevant to the whole. Anton Chekhov maintained that if you mention a gun in the first paragraph, you'd better make sure it is used.

'The end of the world' might seem like a bad choice, but what about three hours in the life of one person preparing for it? This would easily fit a four thousand word limit. So would the day after a divorce settlement, rather than the break-up of the relationship itself; or an incident like the simple first discovery that a husband is playing away from home. In suggesting these two, I've missed out the obvious choice for a novel (fraught people in a meltdown situation) and selected aspects of that situation which could make a convincing short narrative.

Whole films have been based on short stories; *Brokeback Mountain* and *Eyes Wide Shut* owe their origins to a few pages of prose. As you can see, it's not a genre without impact. Meanwhile, historic writers like Katherine Mansfield and O. Henry were famous in their lifetimes for their ability to create perfect short stories.

Aim and Direction

It always helps if your work has a sense of progression, one which keeps the reader engaged. Your plot has to move along from A to Z – a process usually described as 'narrative drive'. Popular novels need a lot of it, as you may know from fast-moving blockbusters and historical sagas. The following paragraphs will help you get to grips with this important facet of writing.

Is something new happening within each chapter or part of your narrative? Has a point of view changed, a problem concluded or begun, another character made their entrance? All of these create narrative drive, giving your book an overall direction to it. The reader knows something is continuing to happen in the background, and while they read, the characters are developing and locations or themes are becoming clearer.

To keep a check on your narrative drive, list how your plot is moving on from one section to the next. It can be simple and brief, like:

1. The mysterious letter is received.
2. A. goes in search of the writer, B.
3. A. finds the address, but B has moved.

In the above example, notice how one thing has led on from another. The ball keeps rolling.

B comes into the story because A has received a letter; A is forced out of his or her normal routine, revealing an inquisitive nature which perhaps we didn't know about previously. In consequence, that character has developed. And the plot thickens when B has failed to appear. We now have an element of suspense – where is B? Why was the letter written? Is someone playing games with A? A narrative with drive is starting up!

Moving On

If you find that nothing has advanced on the previous chapter, you need to think about the direction of your work. Even if you are writing a trilogy and seven chapters are devoted to how your character boils an egg, it is self-indulgent to assume that you don't need narrative hooks to keep the reader with you. Ask yourself: why should a reader be engaged in this? If I wasn't writing it, would I be bothered about what's happening?

If too much of the action is internal (for example, an isolated character's thoughts and feelings) your resulting work may be a little static. The character doesn't move, and nobody speaks to them; nothing intrudes on the scene. Yet a narrative drive can still be obtained by:

> ➢ Having that character respond to time passing.
> ➢ Outside noises, which indicate that other lives are happening around them.
> ➢ Vivid memories or daydreams, which in themselves show narrative progression.

It doesn't have to be crash, bang, wallop. It can be intimate, slow, miniaturist. But something or someone has to shift along; otherwise the reader will switch off.

Yards of description alone will cause the reader to close the covers without delay – something realised by *Cold Comfort Farm* satirist Stella Gibbons, who asterisked her purple passages in advance so that readers could miss them out! So, to keep up the pace and prevent your narrative grinding to a halt, limit the number of purely descriptive passages.

Limiting your description is particularly important for gaining the reader's attention in the first place. Critics often complain that a novel is 'hard to break into' or it 'takes too long to get under way', 'nothing happens until page 40'. In other words, the writer has spent far too long setting the scene when a brisker entry would have been more effective. The narrative drive has been blocked.

Narrative drive is often harder to achieve in poetry outside the usual genre of storytelling in verse. But when you're engaged on a series of poems, it helps if a narrative structure lies behind the work, otherwise your sequence might read as inconclusive and lacking a point to it. Your reader will think 'what was all that about?' instead of admiring how one thing led expertly to another. And that's what narrative drive, aim and direction is all about: one thing leading to another. If you can write some of those, you've got it sorted.

Pointers for You

> Decide where the climax is going to be in your story, and build steadily towards it or away. Think of your chapters like steps.

> If a character isn't helping to move the plot along by their speech or actions, why are they in your piece?

> Murder, mystery, mayhem – readers and editors expect the first death or crime within the first few pages. It's just one of those things that the industry demands.

> Loose endings – if you intend leaving things unclear or poetic at the end, signal it in the rest of your plotting. Readers tend to feel cheated if they are given an unsatisfactory conclusion without good reason.

> Sonnet sequences are a great way of putting narrative drive into poetry. Traditionally, sonnets were used for debates between lovers or to describe the progress of a relationship.

> Moving characters from one room to another, shifting from one day to the next, people meeting up at the same time each week; these are simple ideas for creating narrative drive.

> ➤ Do what Dickens did and end each chapter on a cliff-hanger. Your audience will keep reading.
> ➤ End a chapter in the middle of an incident – it's hard to stop reading at this point.

Practising Narrative Drive

Remember when you were about five years old. Write a few paragraphs or notes about you and your life back then. However, don't invest your little self with any adult thoughts, or look back at yourself across time. Recreate your habits and environment, using the present tense. Write what that five year old would see and do and think about.

Next, reel the film on a little further and think about your later childhood, aged nine to twelve. The thoughts might be a little more developed and the scenery easier to depict. Your world will probably be wider and not so restricted to home.

Next, jump to later adolescence and recreate your experience then. You might be more involved in school and society, experiencing relationships, making plans for the future.

By now, you will have a series of paragraphs or notes showing narrative drive. Your character will have changed or developed, you are taller, you may have moved house, there may be more or fewer members in your family unit; your best friend may be a different one.

Help your works to grow taller in future by investing them with a clear direction.

Conclusions

You've learned about some of the demarcations between poetry and prose.

You've learned what 'genre' is and discovered the importance of genre, including its commercial importance.

You've discovered more about poetic forms and the problems with rhyme.

You've learned about narrative drive in different forms and gained tips on how to invest your work with clear direction.

Tutorial Section

Points for Discussion

1. Which do you prefer, rhyming or unrhymed verse? Why?
2. Why is genre important in contemporary literature? Or don't you believe that it is?
3. How have contemporary media forms, such as film and television, impacted on how authors construct their narratives?
4. How do you feel about the use of stereotypes to convey characters' personalities quickly?

Practice Questions

1. There is at least one other type of sonnet. What are they, and how are they characterised?
2. Carry out the literary equivalent of a SWOT analysis. As a writer, what (and where) are your strengths, weaknesses, opportunities and threats?
3. Practice word associations. What alternative meanings spring to mind when you read the following:

cheap	salary
worthy	undiscovered
desirable	challenging

4. Take your latest piece of creative writing or find a short story on the Internet. Work through a few sides highlighting parts which do not move the action on and could easily be omitted.

4 Becoming a Creative Writer

One Minute Overview

So you've got the foundations right, but what else must you aim for as a writer? This chapter takes you through several important strands involved in the art of writing. These aren't the only components – they are a further selection of building blocks, intended to give you a firm platform for the future. You'll have writing suggestions for most sections, so keep your notepaper handy – it helps if you work through any questions as you go. Some of them are ways into writing, following on points mentioned in Chapter 1; others are explanations of ingredients common to effective literature, which editors and readers will expect to see. Writing is an art form where you need to be fully engaged as a human being. Observing, using your senses, and being willing to stand in another's shoes, are essential traits which you should develop early on if you want to write well and communicate.

Imitation

Before the 19th century, the standard way of learning art and craft was through imitation. Apprentices and beginners followed a studio style and copied the 'master' until they were ready to head out on their own. This system applied to geniuses and mavericks as well as the many run-of-the-mill average practitioners whose works don't form part of the history books. Yet look at what those centuries produced: Leonardo, Vermeer, William Blake.

Writing too had its apprenticeship of sorts. People studied the classical civilisations and learnt to translate Virgil and Homer. They were immersed in the Bible and Shakespeare. As a result, there was nothing they couldn't achieve; three-volume novels, intricate verse-forms, five act plays. For several centuries, English authors imitated the Italian Renaissance authors, borrowing plots and verse forms like mad. Only one of Shakespeare's plays (*The Merry Wives of Windsor*) is thought to be an original plot line devised by the man himself.

You've already tried an example of imitation based on George Herbert. Borrowing authors for a while is a useful way for total beginners to get into writing and experience what writers do. It's also good for people returning to creative writing after years away, or for keeping yourself at it when you haven't any important projects on the go.

Exercise 1

Select an author you admire. What is a typical subject choice for them? What kinds of words do they use – complex or simple? Are their texts rich in imagery? Emotionally engaged, or detached? Are they pushing home a message?

Write down the hallmarks of this person's style: what makes it a work by X instead of Y. Now try your hand at one of their favourite subjects, using the types of words and sentences they might choose.

Exercise 2

The following authors have distinctive styles, voices, and mannerisms. It makes them ideal for imitation exercises. Off you go!

Jane Austen   Oscar Wilde   JRR Tolkien   Angela Carter
Samuel Beckett   Terry Pratchett   Raymond Chandler

You might laugh at the idea of Terry Pratchett being on that list, yet heavily influenced writers' group members can produce pages of it without realising where the influence is coming from. Be one step ahead and know who you're imitating!

Parody

When imitation goes way over the top, parody is the result. You can create this effect easily by taking one or two characteristics from a favourite author and exaggerating them until the subject matter becomes comic and out of control. It works well if the subject is one which the author would never choose under any circumstances. Think how Oscar Wilde would portray an episode of *Eastenders*, for example. Or how Jack Higgins would portray a day of vacuous boredom at the seaside.

Exercise

On separate cards, write the names of authors whose styles you'd like to parody. On another set of cards write a number of situations: here are three to get you started.

- ➢ Trapped in a cable-car.
- ➢ Going on a blind date.
- ➢ Being interviewed for a job in a fish-canning factory.

Put the two sets of cards in separate envelopes and shake them up a few times. Now select a card from each, and begin. Keep the envelopes for a future occasion when you haven't written anything for weeks. You are worried that you don't know anything about fish-canning factories? Then make it up – you're a creative writer. …

Topical subjects parodied in the manner of famous poets or popular songs are an entertaining genre, one which appears in print occasionally. They're also good for performance slots, so it's worth writing a couple of parodies for the inevitable party-piece later on. It's fun to let off steam as a writer.

Once you've had some practice with imitation and parody, you'll have learnt a lot about style. Ultimately you will have your own style, and with any luck it'll be as immediately recognisable as some of the people you've studied, without sounding like them. In not writing as yourself, you've had practise in persona-wearing and character-using – important abilities to have if you intend writing fiction or drama.

Observation

Good writers are great observers. If you love to 'waste time' watching assorted members of the public in their daily rounds, you are halfway towards finding material. In particular, you will learn about convincing dialogue, almost without realising it. So, it pays to become a good listener and watcher from the outset. Are you observant about the world at large? Let the following scenario ease you into a state of watchfulness.

Exercise 1

Supermarket queues are a good place for people-watching without being seen. Look at the gallery of fascinating human types in front and behind you. You might have seen them earlier, staggering around with enormous trolleys. How decisive are they when faced with ten different kinds of bread? Do they like shopping or look as though they hate it? How are they dressed? Do they have children? What happens if a small child has a tantrum?

Now have a look at their checkout items. The self-righteous always love to poke fun at the unhealthy contents of other people's baskets. What about eccentric combinations – twenty bags of sweets, and yellow card – maybe someone is having a party. That woman stocking up with industrial quantities of beans, bacon, eggs and tomatoes is probably the owner of a local guest house.

Pathos and abundance can be implied simply through what the person in front of you dumps on the conveyor-belt. Next time you are in the supermarket, look at your fellow shoppers, and how they behave.

Exercise 2

Take your notebook and go for a walk. On the way, note down exactly what happens and whatever you notice. The weather might be important; you might have impressive buildings or an urban feel to your surroundings. Write down what you overhear, and any unusual sights; what the advertising boards say, how many ducks are on the river, the displays and signs in shop windows.

On your return, you will have the beginnings of a creative walk poem – a technique often used by writing tutors 'in the field'. As you develop in your work, themes and significant moments will become more apparent. Soon you can connect observed items with symbols and allusions.

Exercise 3

Here are some good public areas for you to try:

> ➤ Railway station cafes and waiting areas.
> ➤ Bank Holiday special events.
> ➤ Annual shows or weekly markets.
> ➤ Museums.
> ➤ Bus journeys (no, not car journeys – they're too fast, and it's not a good idea to be thinking about creativity if you're the driver!).
> ➤ Graveyards – for names, dates, period details, hidden lives.

As you'll be aware, the above locations are crowded and busy, or packed with 'things'. People won't notice if you're sitting in a corner with a notebook. Fieldwork should be unobtrusive and anonymous; think how alarmed a subject would be if you were sat directly opposite them in a confined space, describing them and noting down their words!

Engaging the Five Senses

How do you experience the world? More than likely it's through the five senses: sight, touch, hearing, smell, taste. But you'll know straight away that one or two of these predominate, and you may also have one which under-performs. Smell and taste tend to be lower down the list, while people who have all five senses still tend to rely on sight more than anything else, even where it proves unreliable without glasses.

When writing, it's just too easy to rely on sight alone – relying on what you as the author can see with your imagination, combined with observed information, and what you might remember visually. But this is only half of the story. You need those other senses involved before the reader can fully visualise the scene. This doesn't mean overdoing it so that your narrative is clogged with slow-moving sensual detail covering all five available interpretations. It means choosing only the best ways of getting that sensory information across.

Examples

For instance, a city back-street littered with rotting vegetable matter might make an interesting visual description, but it could be the appalling stink which really brings home to the reader how deprived-looking and dirty it is. You need that smell to be included before the reader thinks 'disgusting, slimy, urrgghh'. A quiet Sunday in the country might have its quietness reinforced by the sudden intervention of a distant church bell, or the noise of a single car. Weather can be felt as opposed to seen; unpleasant atmospheres might be so toxic that you can almost taste them.

Readers who know about 'synaesthesia' will be familiar with the idea of our senses as transferable, a state where items normally heard or seen can also be felt and experienced in another way. Meanwhile, musicians frequently describe an individual note as having a corresponding colour, in addition to its expected position as a sound and a dot on a musical scale. And most people will have heard a 'cold' voice, or a lovely 'melted dark chocolate' or 'velvety' voice at some point. A voice can't actually be made out of chocolate – yet you know exactly what that means when you hear it. You can sense that smooth, luxury quality in the sound, yet what we are using are words more attuned to the modes of touch and sight and taste.

All of these are examples of the senses being experienced in another context, one which is very similar to how creative images work in the mind. You know that the voice isn't a colour, yet it describes exactly what the voice feels like; it is both accurate and a creative statement. What does it mean for you as a writer? It means something wholly useful and positive. It means that you can derive creative energy, descriptive power, and a wider range of imagery, simply by involving more of your senses. What's more, just as readers can understand the idea of a 'melted chocolate' voice, the majority of your comparisons will be understood too. It pays to take a few risks.

Exercise 1

What does 'summer' mean to you? Divide your page into five sections and label each with one of the senses. Now write as many sentences as you can, under those headings.

Exercise 2

When you are cooking or watching someone else cook, close your eyes for a couple of minutes and experience the moment through hearing and smell and touch. Afterwards, note down the main impressions you felt. Add the sensation of taste after your meal.

Exercise 3

Go to a department store and experience the smells available at the cosmetics stands and testers.

Slow down!

People are often in a tearing hurry, which blocks out much of what our senses are trying to tell us. Becoming alive to our senses involves slowing down for a period, while taking the trouble to experience the environment. The next time you are in a new place:

> ➤ Notice textures – feel the differences of stone, wood, metal, brick.
> ➤ Examine the different fabrics on your clothing – which textures do you prefer?

> ➤ Listen to a house at night – how noises become magnified and how ordinary creaks and rustles take on that unnerving mystery quality.
> ➤ Rediscover play: this helps to shake up the senses and encourage a new perspective.
> ➤ Try cycling instead of driving – you will notice more about the natural world.

Contrast and Variety

These two will help you create interesting narratives. It's no good having a novel where every scene is populated by carbon-copies who aren't about to change, oppose each other, discover anything, move, or stray from their ordered lives. It would be dull, hard to move along, and difficult for you to create excitement. As for showpiece descriptions, such as of a good climax or an air of suspense and foreboding – these might not fit within your narrative frame if the overall tone of your work is one of Zen-like inaction. For an involving story, you need contrasting characters and different settings, if only to keep the reader with you. Something must happen!

As a classic example of contrast in action, look at the good-cop/bad-cop combination so beloved of crime and TV drama. Reginald Hill's Dalziel and Pascoe books work because the shambolic Dalziel is a good contrast with the family-man Pascoe. In Patricia Cornwell's Kay Scarpetta novels, much is made of the ongoing work relationship between wisecracking tough-nut Marino and the tense, orderly Scarpetta. In both cases, the characters are perfect foils for one another. The narrative lifts when the complementary character appears; when one is carrying the action forward, readers wonder what the other one is doing.

In literature, opposites attract. King Lear has his Fool, Sherlock Holmes has Dr. Watson, angry-man Jimmy Porter has the passive Alice. The sparks fly, plots thicken, and something meaningful is said whenever these combinations appear on the page. That's because experienced writers have learned that 'odd couples' create dramatic tension. And contrasting main characters often like or respect one another because each one supplies the qualities that the other lacks. Many situation comedies work because the main characters are contrasted sharply, making them liable to the adventures and mistakes which keep us laughing.

Variety in scene-setting also helps, because people react differently according to where they are situated. You'll see new facets to a character if, for instance, a spoilt rich girl is sent to work in a deprived borough. It's no accident that audience-grabbing reality TV works on the same premise of contrast and variety. Throw together an assortment of people, put them in an unfamiliar situation, and the resulting inflammatory mix will cause a story.

Contrasting characters are not confined to easy-reading, since heavy-duty literary novels use subtle variations of the same technique. In John Fowles' *The French Lieutenant's Woman*, Victorian Ernestine is contrasted with 'dangerous siren' Sarah, with Charles' reactions causing his downfall or salvation, depending on your point of view. Without this contrast in the two women, there would be no dilemma, no agony, no loss of status and no subterfuge, and fewer occasions for change.

Exercise

Explore the notion of contrast and variety by writing a couple of A4 pages using the following guidelines. Show a few additional characteristics when the location changes.

> ➤ A townie visiting a country person.
> ➤ A pupil versus a teacher, during class and after class.
> ➤ A tourist passing through two locations, one prosperous, the other run-down.
> ➤ A gang leader who also cares for a sick relative.

You'll have realised by now that contrasting characters, particularly if they don't agree or like each other, might lead to a powerful conflict in a story. And the idea of conflict and resolution is another major feature of popular writing, one which you can't do without if your story is meant for others to read.

Conflict and Resolution

There is an obvious conflict situation in any story involving hatred, war, or where characters have to compete with each other; but in literature there are alternative forms. Briefly:

A conflict is any situation or opposing force which prevents our main character from going where he wants to go.

It could be a lifestyle he wants but cannot attain, a problem he tries to overcome, an inbuilt personal failing which trips him up. It could be an assignment he is on, a relationship falling apart, or the fact that a re-occurring person is wrongly perceived as an opponent. In a short story, an old woman could be preoccupied by a dripping tap that keeps her awake all night; a shopper might have a problem finding the right shoes for a wedding. All of these are forms of conflict, because progress is being blocked by something that the character must overcome.

As your hero battles with their nemesis, there will probably be a **climax** somewhere along the line. He may triumph, or not; either way, we should have a **resolution**. The murderer is banged up for life, and the wily inspector dusts herself down and smiles for the first time in three hundred pages. Result! Or the no-hoper who's useless at DIY finally puts together the flat-pack wardrobe. Hooray! In open-ended situations, people might learn a little bit more about themselves before they head towards another dose of the same conflict as before.

A good resolution, no matter how cataclysmic or gentle, will create a feeling of satisfaction and closure. The effort has been worth it, both for the readers and the characters. Your readers will enjoy a good resolution, which ties up the noticeable loose ends … unless your baddie has escaped, ready to cause conflict in the sequel. In some novels there's a winding-down sequence, where we see the main character returning to normal or enjoying a quiet moment after the storm.

Exercise

How would you resolve the following conflicts in a story? Provide some background detail to these exercise pieces, since the conflict must have started somewhere in the past for it to become an issue.

- ➤ Neighbours disputing a hedge boundary.
- ➤ An agoraphobic who refuses to go out.
- ➤ Two brothers who hate each other.
- ➤ A superhero who wakes up one morning to discover that their special powers have gone.
- ➤ An actor who cannot make a successful audition.
- ➤ A young mother left to deal with a difficult child.

Point-of-View

If you're engaged on a prose work, the question of narrative viewpoint might arise. For example, having a traditional all-seeing narrator isn't the only way of writing a story. You could tell the story from an insider's viewpoint – one of the characters involved in the story – maybe the main character, or a bystander who is only partly involved in the action.

But these alternative methods put specific demands on you as an author.

- ➤ You must have that character's personality in mind all the time, since they must speak and relate everything as themselves, not like you would.
- ➤ They will probably have a biased viewpoint, and they can't appear in two places at once.
- ➤ They can't really know what someone else is thinking unless they are told by a confidant.
- ➤ A reader will only see what's happening through that character's eyes; if they're not compelling enough, your reader will be bored.

Using an 'outsider' character might broaden the point-of-view available to the reader. This is because your outsider or bystander can view more than one aspect of what's going on. For instance, they might be related to all the protagonists and they might be a regular visitor; they might be an employee with access to all areas; they might be in charge of the case and possess all the data; or they might be the family cat. Preferably they won't have too much of an axe to grind, then the question of bias won't come up. The reader will experience a wider-ranging viewpoint, provided you are convincing at engineering matters so that your narrator is present at the crucial moments in your story.

An Example

In Alice Sebold's bestseller *The Lovely Bones*, narrator Susie Salmon is dead, talking to us from her new life in heaven. So although the book is largely using a first-person style of narrative, Susie the ghost has the power to see into other people's minds and motives – not to mention an ability to travel anywhere on earth within a flash. The book succeeds because the writer has given herself the widest possible method of following her characters around, while at the same time writing in an engaged manner as one of the people involved. And the reader willingly suspends their disbelief in the proceedings, because we can readily accept the idea of a ghost having superior travelling methods and an attachment to her living relatives.

The next time you are reading a novel or short story, think about who this mysterious 'I' figure might be. If it's not an omniscient narrator, why do you think that particular viewpoint was chosen? What advantage does this chosen persona have as opposed to another character in the book?

How About You?

There is another point of view – yours. Nineteenth-century novelists like Trollope and Dickens occasionally make an appearance in their own works, often for moralising reasons, which would be unacceptable in literature today. Experimental novelists sometimes pop in for a lark, or because they're fabricating different versions of themselves for artistic reasons. John Fowles was notorious for appearing in *The French Lieutenant's Woman*, and for providing two different endings. Such methods are attractive to writers who like to play with the artificial and multi-layered nature of literature.

If in doubt about which point of view to use or whether you should limit yourself at all, remember that it's easier to have an all-seeing unnamed narrator, the godlike traditional teller of stories. Its particular advantage is that it allows you to express your own individuality, as opposed to channelling your talent through another mouthpiece.

Building a Character

So many stories fail because the characters are unbelievable or simply not engrossing enough. As a reader, you might have come across a well-hyped novel where the supposedly charismatic main character is far less deep, sexy, witty and wide-ranging than the people you see on the street outside. If you've ever criticised lacklustre characterisations, you're half way towards making better ones of your own. Earlier sections will have mentioned that using real-life models can be a short-cut to successful literary people, but – what happens if nobody you know fits the ideas you have in mind, or the model you are using needs to change radically?

When creating believable people, you need to perform the paper equivalent of method acting. When actors take on a role, they frequently study the background and motivation of the person they're portraying – yes, even if most of the resulting information doesn't end up having an actual place in the play. That's because a character has to be made three-dimensional with emotions and history before the actor can really feel what's going on.

Get To Know Your People

By understanding a character before it enters your story on paper, you'll be one step closer to succeeding. Therefore, make out the following checklist for every important character:

    Full name and any previous name
    Brief outline of appearance
    Place of birth, parents' occupations

Schooling and favourite subjects

College or training

First jobs

Partner and/or significant friends, relationships

Hobbies and interests

Likes and dislikes

Notable achievements, notable low points

Where they want to be in ten years' time.

After providing your characters with a CV, note down how they become involved with the action in your book. 'She lives next door' is too vague, but 'she moved here to escape from an abusive ex-husband who was stalking her' might account for why she never appears after 6pm and never answers the door … leading to a crucial reason for something else, later in the story.

Now things are starting to look plausible; we know why this character behaves the way she does, and details can be drip-fed to the reader as a means of adding depth to your narrative.

It might also help you if a speech sample is given. Your background details may provide clues about how this character might sound, even if you have no idea of their actual voice at the start. Accent, forcefulness and intelligence can all affect a person's choice of words and how they come out of the mouth. A typical sentence or two might provide a reference point if you start to lose your grip later on!

Habits and Hooks

A few human quirks and 'hooks' might help your characters to live on the page. Annoying habits peculiar to that person, like hair-fiddling or ring-twisting; the way they sit or stand, fast or slow walking – all of these are believable human traits which can be reproduced on the page, adding up a catalogue of detail which presents a whole picture. Someone with a non-Western name might be forever spelling it out when dealing with not-very-bright officials. Different cultural backgrounds are often a big determining factor in how your cast-members think about themselves. Give them sports or hobbies, something which they might have done before they came to be involved in your work.

What, do I mean to say that your characters think about themselves? Aren't they just non-existing figments of a godlike writer's imagination? No, not any more – start treating them like real people instead of cardboard cutouts, and they might start doing things with real conviction on the page. Don't be afraid to daydream about what a 'resting' character might be doing while off the scene – your ideas may turn out to be useful later in your narrative.

Exercise

What characteristics would you use to portray the following people?

> - A vulgar, brassy, but sympathetic middle-aged woman.
> - A young man who finds it hard to make friends.
> - A salesperson with a go-getter attitude who regularly achieves their targets.

> **Study Tip**
>
> Characters sometimes take over. You envisage their voices clearly, and whatever they say magically looks right on the page. This is excellent news for you as author. Go with the flow and let them have some room. If you ever reach the stage where you feel like a reporter taking down scenes unfolding in front of you and happening one after the other, this is ideal.

Plotting and Planning

Let's look at why you need a plot in the first place. You need one because creative stories are made up from incidents and actions, characters who have lives, causes which lead to effects. Because of X, Y happens, and because of Y, Z happens. If you're not in control of this process, your writing will lack tension, or sufficient narrative drive, or adequate organisation … or all three. Things will happen for no reason, actions will have no consequences, and the chain of cause and effect will be broken. A jumbled mass of unrelated incidents doesn't make a story – there has to be something binding it together. This is where your plot, structure, or governing ideas come in.

Spend a few minutes on the Internet and you'll find plenty of advice. Some authors claim that there are only seven different plots in the world, while others stretch this to ten or twelve. Apparently there are thirty-six dramatic situations. Or only three basic narratives from which all the others develop. I don't know about you, but I'm confused already. The only plot which matters is the one you are going to write, and while it might be based on an archetype from long ago, the plot should be a) plausible within the scope of the book and the characters, and b) well written. You can get away with quite a lot, so long as a) and b) are in place. You should definitely avoid:

> Far-fetched and ridiculous coincidences as a way of solving plot issues.

> Rich relatives suddenly dying and leaving the destitute heroine a legacy out of the blue (this and the preceding one are so Victorian).

> Actions which are out of character for the people you are writing. Yes, addictions and mental problems can result in out-of-character actions, but you need to provide some hints and foreshadowing first, if that's what happens!

> Vital evidence which appears out of nowhere at the last minute, connected to nothing and nobody, and which the detectives couldn't possibly miss if they'd known.

> Lack of momentum. Long stories and novels will flow in peaks and troughs, but you don't want incidents spread too thinly across your narrative, as this will bore readers.

> Ending on 'and then I woke up and it was all a dream'. This was old news in the fourteenth century. It's also a cheat ending, since it means you can drop any difficult plot situation without having to explain anything.

> ➢ Giving the game away too early in your narrative – or the rest of the story will be an anticlimax.
> ➢ Technology block – remember that mobile phones, broadband, DNA testing and other recent advances will affect how your characters find evidence and connect with the world.

How Much Working Out?

Some writers have everything worked out in advance, down to the last detail. They have maps and diagrams on their walls, and flowcharts to show plot movements. Others can't bear the thought of knowing so much at the outset, preferring to discover the plot themselves as they write it. It doesn't matter which method you prefer – one is not 'right', the other 'wrong'. As a beginner, it might be worth trying both methods to see which one works for you.

A rough outline may be all you need to prevent a book from going off the rails, without killing off your spontaneity by over-planning. I've often noted briefly 'what comes next' in the margins of a handwritten first draft. Even if you don't know exactly what happens in the end, it helps if you have a general direction in mind. A brief diagram or rough note will keep you focused, particularly if you have a deadline or limited time to write the whole book. Writers in genres with intricate storylines – family sagas, crime, historical adventures – will usually need a few timescales or family trees to help them along.

Devices and Other Mechanisms

While you're engaged on your story, you might need a few devices to control your information and how much gets through to the reader. Handy literary items for your plots include:

> ➢ Foreshadowing – planting information which heralds an important point later on.
> ➢ Dramatic irony – for example, someone insisting that things are fine when we know from other events that they're about to become worse.

> ➤ Secrets and hidden information – characters who prevent things becoming known.
> ➤ Reversal – for example, those with power lose it, those without, gain it.
> ➤ Flashbacks.
> ➤ Different viewpoints describing the same incident – so that the reader builds up a picture which isn't known to one or more of the characters.
> ➤ Recurring symbols and themes; music, geography, unfinished works, growing plants – all of these could punctuate your plot with their added significance.
> ➤ Weather and landscape features, which reflect feelings and atmospheres in the story.

As an author, you are responsible for what happens in the book – what the reader sees and understands is your business. You're not just a creator of characters and situations, but the reporter, art director, stage manager and photographer as well, not to mention the resident psychiatrist and the house critic when the lights resume at the end of the show.

Sub-Plots

Alongside your main plot – let's say 'the hero's difficult personal journey' – you might want a sub-plot. This provides a contrast to the main action while at the same time being relevant and engrossing in its own way – let's say 'the hero's sister realises that her much-loved brother is losing touch with reality'. Plots can run in a parallel manner (for example, similar events but different characters, historic time vs. present time) or against the grain; but one thing is certain. It can't overwhelm the main plot. If this occurs during your first draft, it might be useful to swap the plots around so that your strongest one becomes the book. In my brief example above, the sister's plot line could easily take over when she realises that she must undergo a difficult journey of her own.

Some writers are generous souls who blitz the reader with multiple plot lines; others use one sparse plot line and still achieve stunning results. In Magnus Mills' *The Restraint of*

Beasts, one idea is stretched to the limit, yet it never becomes boring due to the black humour and carefully placed surprises. Sub-plots are therefore not essential to the success of a story, but you still need enough variety in characters or situations for the reader to stay engaged.

Basic Plots and Ideas

As a means of starting to write, old archetypes are valuable. You can hang your story on any one of them, and providing your narrative isn't too formulaic, it's hard to fail. That's why authors have continued to use them over the centuries. If you explore ancient myths, other plot lines will come to light; in *45 Master Characters*, the author makes use of the Babylonian Astarte myth from the Epic of Gilgamesh. That's quite a change from the usual Greek and Roman storehouse.

Here are some of those archetypal plots for you to think about:

> ➢ The hero or heroine embarks on a journey or quest (the Odyssey, Don Quixote).
> ➢ From rags to riches (Cinderella).
> ➢ Growing up and coming of age/maturing into adulthood (the Bildungsroman).
> ➢ A hero or heroine is faced with an impossible dilemma.
> ➢ The hero or heroine has a fatal flaw which causes their downfall (classic tragedy).
> ➢ Partners meet, lose each other, and then meet again with changes having occurred (classic romance).
> ➢ Human versus the environment, whether natural or man-made.
> ➢ The mysterious stranger who rides into town.
> ➢ The trickster who causes chaos wherever he goes.

Experimental novels have been written where readers can select their own random plots by shuffling loose chapters in a box. This sounds like cutting edge literature, yet the author has still provided a range of options and outcomes in the first place. In short, you can be as experimental as you like, but there must be a plot of some kind. Believable stories will always contain these two principles:

Cause and Effect.   *Action and Reaction.*

Without these, you don't have a plot.

Good Middles and Satisfying Ends

Successful writing must always start well. You'll be learning about effective starting techniques in the next chapter, because arresting starts are often a big problem for new writers and it helps if you know several tried and trusted ways into a text. But successful narratives also need a middle that doesn't sag and an ending which is worth waiting for. As implied previously, you can't get far without that satisfying sense of closure in your story – the same one you feel when you have read a novel by an established author. Typical reader responses would be 'I'm glad the heroine achieved her goal' or 'What a moving and brilliant final episode'. Character-centred works might involve a new understanding or a true perspective instead of a false one.

Writing the middle section is laborious, as you may discover when tackling anything longer than 4,000 words. You might feel as though you're wading through swampy ground, slowed down and directionless, with nothing except more of the same in front of you. Or: what if you've got beyond the start, set your chickens flying … and you know how the chickens come home to roost in the end … but you don't know what happens to the birds in the meantime? This is where knowing your characters and doing some advance plotting really pays off. Otherwise, your narrative will peter out and you may lose interest in the work – the classic point where new writers give up and where rewrites prove difficult and boring. Even experienced writers pack up halfway through when they've become lost in the swamp.

While writing the middle section, consider the following:

> ➢ What do you want from the middle of a book? Note down those things which usually keep you interested in a narrative.

> ➢ How are your characters behaving and reacting? What's their next move?
> ➢ Who are their friends and opponents? How do they react to any changes?
> ➢ What is everyone trying to achieve? How are they going to do it?
> ➢ Are your events – weather, violence, accidents – looking plausible within the overall conditions of your story?
> ➢ Don't resort to making things happen without good reason, just to keep the narrative going. You might be tempted, but the end result will look disjoined and you will lose that essential cause and effect momentum described earlier.

Set goals for your cast and ensure they have made some progress after a while. Above all, regard your middle chapters as steps or stages, leading the reader towards another level. Your keyword to remember is 'development', whether for characters, action sequences, or both.

Exercises

You can analyse novels to see where the authors place their significant moments and new stages in the narrative, but it's best if you have some practice at writing some middle parts yourself. So here are five instant exercises to give you some familiarity with moving from A to B. For each example, provide five or more interim stages between the middles and the ends as provided.

Exercise 1

Beginning: The hero is born in the wrong part of town, and his parents don't like him.
End: He achieves a relationship with his own children and wins back his estranged partner.

Exercise 2

Beginning: An alien lands on Earth.
End: The alien decides to stay on Earth.

Exercise 3

Beginning: Rich, popular, and beautiful; the only way was down.
End: Her agent rushes to the hospital, but it's too late.

Exercise 4

Beginning: Three children discover a magic carpet.
End: The owner of the carpet finally catches up with them.

Exercise 5

Beginning: A team of misfits must rescue a colleague trapped in an enemy dungeon.
End: Back at HQ the survivors receive their medals.

Study Tip

When engaged on your own literature in future, you might find that a time line will help. Sometimes, writers calculate the overall time they are covering – whether a few hours or several years – and then place their series of significant plot moments along a drawn line, with dates or days as needed. If you find that everything is bunching up at the wrong end of your line, your narrative needs help!

A Challenge: Try Reading This

Some of our most eccentric novels still follow the beginnings, middles and ends tradition. In Laurence Sterne's *Tristram Shandy* – a story usually held up as being original and 'postmodern' before the term was even invented – the author begins with Tristram's parents like any conventional autobiography. And it ends with the major characters enjoying a storytelling session together, in a reflection of the book's wider purpose as a lengthy 'cock and bull' story. Consequently, there is a satisfying closure even though the author has done everything he can to drive us all around the houses during the preceding pages. *Tristram Shandy* was first published in 1760, and it's hard to beat for sheer inventiveness. What happens to the 'middle' in this narrative? How does Sterne keep going?

Show, Don't Tell

In workshops and writing courses you will often hear the instruction 'Show, don't tell', yet this is one of the hardest things for people to accomplish. Examples are difficult to find, since already-published writers are succeeding on the basis that they're doing it right. They're already showing, not telling. Meanwhile, inexperienced writers will regard their narrative as expressly designed to tell/show the reader what was intended. It means what it says, they will argue. 'I've explained exactly what I meant. This says what I meant it to say. What's wrong with it?'

The simplest explanation is that **showing** the reader allows them to experience the story using their senses and imaginations, making the whole reading experience richer and more meaningful. On the other hand, **telling** the reader what to think, say and experience from the outset is a style trait which throws up barriers. The reader is being talked at, and the writer's tone of voice may be too didactic and flat in addition.

An Example

'It was cold in the waiting room where Harold sat down' is closer to telling. I'm stating something from above, setting the scene and moving Harold in like a toy-theatre figure on a stick. This might be all right as a scene-setter, but it's also bland and not particularly engrossing for a reader. 'Harold climbed back into his overcoat and rubbed his hands together' is closer to showing. Harold is doing something on his own behalf which suggests that the temperature is minus centigrade. If I'd continued with ice visible around the window frame and a benefits assistant wearing sheepskin gloves behind a bolted-on Perspex hatch, you would know it was a cold room along with other relevant information, like institutional and unfriendly. It may even be colder than outside. And the reader is being led into a story, as opposed to being told a couple of facts.

Using the senses will be instrumental in showing rather than telling. So will active forms of language rather than passive. If you re-read the brief example given above, the 'telling' sentence is passive and only one basic idea is being conveyed. In the 'showing' example, there is movement and motivation as well as a temperature issue. You know what an overcoat looks like – and this one must be heavy or long, because Harold has to climb into it. Which means that Harold could be shortish, old, or not very dextrous. See? A greater range of associations and clues will arise from a passage where 'showing' figures larger than 'telling'.

Another example

Janet was born in 1961. She felt that her life was full of missed opportunities and suspected that she looked older than she was. When her fifteen-year-old daughter Sophie trotted up to her carrying an art folder one day, the insolent girl had asked whether she'd been a Mod or a Rocker.

'The insolence of it! I mean, the sheer assumption! I'm not your grandmother's age, I'm only in my early forties for heaven's sake. Do I look that old? No, of course I wasn't a Mod or a Rocker … stupid … what's it for anyway, some school thing? Sophie – don't walk off like that, you've forgotten your art folder'.

In this example, the second passage sounds livelier and conveys similar information without the same extent of 'telling'. We're not told directly that Janet feels concerned about ageing, yet this attitude comes across when she sounds annoyed at her daughter for mixing up her twentieth century fashions. As a starting point for a short story, this second one involving direct speech would have a stronger impact, because character and emotion is portrayed along with the information. This episode is showing, not telling.

Exercise

It could take ages for you to find noticeable examples of 'telling, not showing' in a novel or short story. Therefore, compile a sample paragraph of your own – rewriting it to give a greater number of sentences which 'show'.

Editing Your Work

When writers complete a first draft – that is, a manuscript or typescript with all the bits they want to include – it's not the end of the creative process. Some new writers believe that their first drafts are complete works of art and fit to show around, only to discover that other people disagree. The first step you must always take is:

> Put your work in a drawer or file and don't touch it for at least a week.

At last, you can start all those things you've been promising yourself once 'it' was finished.

On your return to the script, certain problems will stand out immediately. Look for:

- A rocky, uncertain start instead of a confident opening passage.
- Typographical errors (called 'typos' in the trade) and spelling mistakes.
- Undeveloped descriptions.
- Pacing problems – some parts read too fast, others drag or feel aimless.
- Abrupt, jumpy transitions from one paragraph to another.
- Jumbled sense which needs re-ordering.
- Omissions – you passed over some sentences when typing from notes.
- Repetitions – the same phrase or word used within the same paragraph.

> ➢ Rushed endings – everything concluded within a few lines as though you've run out of material or just given up.

You'll find others which apply to your style and subjects, but the ones I've listed above are common. Distancing yourself from your script is necessary at this stage; it's almost impossible for anyone to tell where the mistakes are while they are engrossed on a project, but once a few days have passed, the inconsistencies will rise to the surface. You might not believe me if this is your first attempt at sustained creative writing, so the best thing to do is … try it and see.

You are now involved in the editorial process. If you've left plenty of space around your text, write your corrections and additions in red pen, using these margins. Otherwise, you'll have to insert numbered sheets near the affected areas.

Study Tip

Try not to end up with a Chinese puzzle-box of interleaved and pasted-on pages. This will be miserable to type out and you might cause a second level of omissions and mixtures!

More Revision

Once you've had a chance to correct any mistakes, return to the beginning and see what can be improved.

> ➢ Passages or words which add nothing to the direction of your script – redundant words, pointless episodes, anything which distracts from the flow of your story. Ask whether they should come out completely, or whether it is possible to rewrite them so that they do fit the story you are trying to tell.
> ➢ Inconsistent descriptions – appearances which change without reason, relative heights of characters, etc. Can your 5 ft heroine really lift that broadsword or see over that wall?

➤ Timing – if your character has to complete something crucial within a limited time and then arrive at another location shortly after, make sure this is possible within the time frame you have given them!

Yes, there's a lot to think about. After the writing process, you become like the continuity staff on your own film. If you've described a room and said that the door is next to a wardrobe, it's no use having it change position during the course of your book, unless the householder has moved address. Noisy incidents which are somehow not noticed by neighbours – are your reasons plausible?

Once you've struck out the parts you don't need and inserted the new improved ones, it's time to finalise your second draft. This is where it all comes together as a work of art, and if you're very lucky, it might well be your final version. However, long and complex literature, high-concept novels, research based history and the like, may need further drafts. It's not unusual for novels to start out as third-person narratives, only for the second draft to be in first-person narrative.

Decide what is best for your book, not what is most convenient for you at the time!

Poets are fortunate compared to prose writers – you may be dealing with one sheet of paper while they are considering hundreds. But the same procedure applies. Is your first line suitably arresting? If not, it should go. Consistency matters if you are a rhyming-verse poet – see the **problems with rhyme** section in Chapter 3. What is the overall point of your poem – dazzling description, a message, an insightful moment, a memory, a good laugh? Is this clear enough?

New poets often write 'chopped up prose', paying little attention to rhythm and image. Is it better off as a short story? If bordering on the prosaic, is it sufficiently insightful and different from prose for it to qualify as a poem?

Above all, treat editorial work as another stage in the creative process, not like an add-on extra, which is nothing to do with you or your initial ideas. The first stage of editorial work is always up to you.

> **Study Tips**
> Here's what to do with poor starting lines.
> Often, the second paragraph is a better place to begin. Or, an unused notebook line contains the exact associations you might need. Or... the perfect opening paragraph might arise as you write the conclusion. Always wait until you are fully engaged on your work before sorting this one out. Worrying about the start while you're still there might stop you from writing beyond page two.

More editing – Sharpening the Focus

Apart from the broad points mentioned above, you might need to look at your phrasing again. Search out the lame and imprecise phrases in your stories; things like 'it was really nice', 'he didn't feel very good', 'it wasn't that impressive', 'it was lovely'. Good storytelling is about making the reader see what you want them to see. This means precise phrasing, accurate descriptions according to your individual vision, and avoiding vague words which don't really tell us what's going on! If you re-read the sample phrases I've given above, you will notice that none of them tell us much about what we might want to know. What, exactly, is 'nice'? Just how bad was it when he 'didn't feel very good'? If something wasn't impressive, what was it instead? Phrases we might use in casual conversation, and those we scribble on our holiday postcards, are not the same as those we should use when storytelling.

It's just as easy for you to find precise, descriptive alternatives. 'Hot weather, empty beaches' instead of 'nice', and 'he threw up on the ferry' add so much more to the picture, even though there's no complicated artistry going on, no difficult images, nothing which a complete beginner would find impossible. Weak phrasing in your narrative writing will make your story dull and the reader won't feel involved. Therefore, once your first draft is complete, replace anything flat and non-committal which doesn't contribute to the overall picture. Your story will suddenly jump into life and lose that out-of-focus impression – almost as though your imagination has put on a much more suitable pair of glasses.

Of course, you can create the impression of a bored character by using exactly the sort of imprecise, tepid wording in their speech lines which your narrative parts should avoid. Their flat, uninterested phrasing will say plenty to the reader! 'Oh, I haven't really noticed. Yes, it was nice'.

> **Study Tip**
> Using negatives – wasn't, didn't, isn't – is usually an ineffective way to describe something. It's quicker and livelier to say what something *is*.

Conclusions

You've become experienced at observing people like a writer, and you have experimented with some different styles in writing.

You've learnt that variety and conflict are important elements in a creative story, and that it's necessary to have believable characters with some depth to their personalities.

You've discovered where to find some strong starter plots if your own ideas aren't yet engrossing enough.

While showing is a great deal harder to do than telling, it's one of the most important things you can learn, no matter what genre you are in.

You've learnt how important it is to edit your work.

Tutorial Section

Points for discussion

1. What plotlines and character stereotypes are available to you through your cultural background?
2. How would you disguise stock characters so that they appear more realistic in a contemporary setting?
3. How would you integrate the 'sixth sense' into literature?
4. This beginning, middles and ends thing – isn't it just old-fashioned?

Practice questions

1. Turn to the Internet and discover how many plot situations are suggested by online resources. Note down the ones you could use.
2. Record a conversation between people you know, and transcribe the conversation exactly how it sounds. How does your result differ from conversations in stories?
3. Devise a rounded pair of characters who would represent the idea of contrast and variety.
4. How many killer opening lines can you write within 45 minutes?

Avoiding Common Mistakes

In the previous chapters, you've already learned to avoid some of the problems which happen to creative writers. You have discovered the most common grammatical mistakes and how to correct them, and you have worked through some exercises and discovered more about the process of writing. But there are other difficulties which might hold you back as a new writer – and this chapter is designed to rid you of those before it's too late to change. Being honest about yourself and your writing is essential at this stage.

Therapy or Writing?

Many people turn to creative writing as an outlet for coping with medical issues or a difficult life. Social pressures too can result in a need for writing as therapy – stress, depression and loneliness are all powerful reasons why anyone would start writing, and you may be familiar with the image of an isolated child who becomes a writer because it provides an escape. You may also come across people with mental health concerns who are encouraged to write as a means of liberating uncomfortable thoughts. Writing is used to connect with humanity, explain away problems, and deal with obsessions.

But there is a big difference between writing as therapy and writing as literature, and it's one of attracting and keeping an audience. Therapy is private, whereas literature is public. If you are coming to creative writing through the therapy route, bear in mind that the same subject matter may be too personalised and offputting for an outside reader. What is suitable for the support group and therapist is probably not suitable for a reader or an editor. If you've ever been cornered by a relative who likes nothing more than to talk about her operations at length, you'll see what I mean. Just because it's you and not this tedious relative doesn't make it any different!

Making it Work – Some Examples

While other sufferers might learn from your experiences, the wider world will probably not find your script attractive unless elements of storytelling, character, and dialogue are included. The 'misery memoir' is currently popular because authors like Frank McCourt (*Angela's Ashes*) are such great storytellers, and they are able to balance the misery with humanity and humour.

Moreover, the runaway success of Mark Haddon's *The Curious Incident of the Dog in the Night-Time* is down to its clever characterisation and bittersweet plot. You learn about autism as a by-product of the story. Christopher Boone's condition is used as a means of exposing the hypocrisy of so-called 'normal' people. The autistic boy is unable to lie, whereas the adults around him construct elaborate fictions to avoid facing the truth. This is a literary novel telling us about false values in our society, rather than a therapy piece.

The same is true of 'confessional' poets. When you read Sylvia Plath or Robert Lowell, you can't help but realise that they experienced the grip of depression and disorder at some point in their lives. But they did more than write about themselves – they tell us what it's like to be alive and with a powerful imagination, as one would expect of a major poet. They write about life, children, history, beekeeping, and relationships – not just their disorders.

If you are using therapy pieces in your work, it might help to consider the following:

> ➤ Using a character or persona (as opposed to yourself) might give you more scope.
> ➤ What can the reader learn from the experiences you depict?

> ➢ How did you overcome difficulties and prejudice? Show people a route that they can take.
> ➢ If you feel apart from society, how can you use this to write better literature as opposed to therapeutic pieces? Are you given a unique perspective on society as an observer?
> ➢ Spontaneous writing while in a state of confusion or depression might provide good material for dramatic monologues and poems later.
> ➢ Avoid droning on at length about symptoms; it will make you sound self-obsessed, even if your words are true.
> ➢ Humour is a good way of keeping the reader on your side.

It's all about angling your work and making it relevant to the 'outside'; seeing the positive uses of a negative period instead of expecting any therapeutic writing to be complete in itself. If you have a special interest in creative writing and health matters, both Lapidus and the Survivor's Poetry movement may be useful to you – their website addresses are given in the bibliography.

Archaism

Here is a definition of archaic: 'out of date or old-fashioned, no longer in everyday use' (Collins Paperback English Dictionary). Yet every day, writers pepper their scripts with language that belongs in the museum. Amateur poets still use o'er, 'tis, wot, and ne'er as if they were living in the nineteenth century, believing it to be 'poetic' language when (sadly) it renders their work laughable. If you're a young writer it's unlikely you will make such a terrible mistake, but older beginners may be tempted to recall the language they absorbed when they first encountered poetry at school many years ago. Don't do it!

The same can be said of inverted word order. You may have read historic examples where poets reverse the last few words in a line so that they fit the rhyme scheme. Unfortunately this will get your work rejected nowadays, and it's advisable not to use inverted word order unless you are Yoda in the Star Wars series, and even then *silly it sounds, when on paper written it is.*

Beginner poets sometimes use combinations of archaic and inverted diction in their efforts to fit the rhyme and remain metrically regular: using 'he did go' instead of 'he went', or 'she did appear' instead of 'she appeared', for example. Again, avoid this at all times, since readers can tell you're not trying too hard. If it happens too often in your work, stop rhyming and try free verse for a while. Change the whole line so that it fits, and never use out of date tenses for the sake of a rhyme.

Contorted words are often found in folk-song verses, where early songwriters had to fit their words around pre-existing tunes, and vice versa. But it often didn't matter in performance, where emotion, lengthened vowels, plentiful real ale, and authentic sound was carrying the listeners over the bumps! Written poetry is an exposing medium, which demands some concentration from the reader. Therefore, old-fashioned word order and clumsy inversions have no place in a modern poem.

What About Period Drama?

Archaic language may be necessary in a historical novel, and the following debate between writers will always be an interesting one. Should we let our characters talk like people 'back then' or give them a modern demotic to speak, bearing in mind that the language of any period is always changing? What's even more confusing is that old words can reappear in a different context (think of 'gay') and some modern-sounding terms could have been in use much earlier than you think.

The safest rule is: if you're not an expert in the period, then become one, as otherwise your characterisation will let you down. Manners, expectations, and behaviour have changed over the centuries even if people have always desired and felt the same things. If you choose a sensible compromise like a contemporary-based non-period speech, a few knowledgeable period terms will make all the difference. The audience will *believe*.

There are dictionaries of historic slang to start you off – these will help you to sort your jakes from your bog house. Useful glossaries are found at the back of school texts in medieval English. The romance writer Georgette Heyer is reliable for Regency language if you find Jane Austen and her contemporaries to be too forbidding. Meanwhile, you can't beat a list of Shakespearian or Jacobean insults for their manic joy in language and its capabilities. All of these simple routes will bring you closer to people of the past. Contemporary novelists like Sarah Waters (*Fingersmith*) and A.S. Byatt (*Possession*) are noted for their command of period settings.

You need a deep love of your chosen period if you want to succeed in historical writing, because many of your readers will share the same period interests. They'll instantly know when you've got it wrong – what's worse, they will write and complain to your publisher! Read everything you can about your period. Politics, brand-names, fashion and transport were just as important then as they are now Look at:

➤ What qualities people prized.
➤ Where they gained their moral guidance.
➤ How were women addressed and treated?
➤ Who represented power and authority?

Writers can fail because they haven't grasped the politics-and-power aspects of their period. It's all too easy to forget that people didn't have the vote until the mid-nineteenth century!

> **Study Tip**
> Slang is now available online at:
> www.dictionaryofslang.co.uk

Cliché and Stereotype

A cliché is a phrase, idea or image, which is so regularly used in speech or writing that it is too banal and obvious for literary purposes. 'Thinking outside the box', 'a roller coaster of emotions', 'at this moment in time', 'dry as dust' and 'quiet as a mouse' are a few examples of clichés. As a result, your work won't sound fresh, interesting or original if more than a couple of them creep unknowingly into your work. The only suitable place for a cliché is when you're depicting a character of limited horizons who gets by on well-worn phrases – otherwise readers will assume you lack a sufficiently wide word-pool of your own. Since many clichés are disguised as similes ('like a bat out of hell') it's important to keep them out of poems, where originality really matters.

Stereotypes are characters or situations which are similarly over-used and therefore unconvincing in print; tall, dark and handsome heroes, blonde bombshells, lazy students and boring accountants are all examples of stereotyped characters. They are two-dimensional, cartoon-like, and not true to life. Yet fiction has thrived on stereotypes to some extent – where would romantic comedy be without its boy meets girl scenario, and what's the point of a pantomime without a baddie to hiss and boo? And where would thrillers be without the hero versus an unspecified-evil-corporation which is threatening to destroy the West?

The secret lies in adequately disguising any stereotypes so that they have more depth and history to their characters. Then, your audience has the satisfaction of combining some familiarity with your original slant on the matter – happily, this is how most genre fiction works. An action hero needn't be a square-jawed man of iron willpower. He could be female, for a start. Or seventy-five and a wheelchair user. Because there aren't any limits; only the ones you are imposing on yourself by following stereotypes too closely. How many stereotyped people do you know in real life?

Stream of Consciousness – Right or Wrong?

'Spontaneous Me' wrote Walt Whitman – but this doesn't mean to say that he shovelled down whatever came into his head and described it as poetry. When you see examples of 'stream of consciousness' writing in classic literature, it's nearly always the result of immense effort from the author, who has made a determined attempt to inhabit a character and describe their thought processes from the inside. For a great example, see the last few pages of *Ulysses* by James Joyce, for Molly Bloom and her famous monologue.

'Stream of consciousness' writing is when you tell a story by thinking with the end of the pen, your random thoughts and incidentals being borne along in the flood. Although the result may look fluent on paper, there will be no organisation to it, with no logical progression from one item to the next. Typically, it will sound jumbled and breathless; sentences will often be long, with little punctuation. Subjects carry equal weight, irrespective of their real importance and dramatic potential – a relaxing bath is written at the same pitch as a car crash. There may be no paragraphs either, and connecting words would typically be repetitive: 'and then I did this, and then I did that'.

Why it Doesn't Work – and What to Do About It

For several reasons, such a writing style will be no use to you in the long term. This is because:

> ➢ Characters, contrast, pacing, and ideas will be lost in the general verbal assault.
> ➢ Everything is at the same pitch (usually fast and furious).
> ➢ It may sound as though a child has written it – which is probably not what you intended.
> ➢ It may result in long slabs of narrative, which the reader finds impenetrable.
> ➢ You may fall into the trap of relating incidents instead of showing a story.

But the worst feature for you as a working writer is this:

> ➢ It leaves you with nowhere to go. All your creativity is up front and there's nothing in reserve. Ideas are used up at a rapid rate and a potential novel will be over within fifty pages.

Stream of consciousness is not acceptable if it's the only style you are using. If you're stuck in this rut, consider the following:

> ➤ What are the important things you are trying to say? Foreground these and describe them to a greater extent on your next draft.
> ➤ Organise your sentences referring to the same thing – clump them together in the same paragraph, or nearby.
> ➤ Slow down your narrative with a few more commas, and take the time to explain.
> ➤ If characters are involved, make sure they sound like separate identities with their own individual thoughts and particular sentences to say, not all the same as you.

Don't panic! There are occasions when stream of consciousness is an effective technique. You might want a dream sequence or a hyperactive dizzy person who can't concentrate for long. As a point of interest within a larger narrative, it can lend insight and originality to your story.

The Right Register

If you listen to different groups of people talking, you will soon discover their range of subjects, their group behaviour, and their choice of language. The latter is what we mean when we talk of 'register'. A businessman at the office will probably not talk to his colleagues in the same way that he communicates with his family back at home; he will be operating, during the day, two different language registers. Someone brought up on the streets will probably not use the same jargon as someone from a public school; and in most cultures, an educated person will sound different from an uneducated one. How does this affect your writing?

Quite simply, it means you have to use the right register if you want your created characters or writing personae to sound convincing. You may have seen films where the lead is miscast, resulting in an unconvincing portrayal and bad reviews. Exactly the same is going to happen in your writing if, for example, you try to depict a top underworld criminal but he sounds and behaves as though he'd be more comfortable running a village teashop. You've used the wrong register; he doesn't sound realistic, and your story will suffer as a result. People prefer to fit in with their social groupings, and will tend to, consciously or subconsciously, adopt the mannerisms and speech patterns of others in their circle. Fail to take this into account, and you will be writing too many inconsistencies.

But wrong registers, as implied, can be used to signal people who are uncomfortable with their position in life, or displaced from where they should be. It can add a layer of subtlety to your story, and provide wry humour. Moreover, if you can successfully write as a persona who is completely unlike yourself, deliberately using the 'wrong' register can become a great test of skill. In *Bleak House*, Dickens took the brave step of writing as a female character for a large part of the book.

As an example of register control, see Alan Bennett's *Talking Heads* monologues. Here, characters with plenty to say but no self-awareness often outline their perceived position in society or their displacement from it, with admirable accuracy and economy.

Exercise

To understand the idea of registers, choose two examples from opposite ends of the literary spectrum – a 'genteel' novel (Barbara Pym, 'Miss Read', Joanna Trollope) and a popular crime novelist (Ian Rankin, Ruth Rendell, Kathy Reichs) and look at (a) the type of speech these contrasting authors use, and (b) the frequency of slang, work jargon, or incomplete dialogue. Do the characters sound realistic? Can you imagine people like that?

Writing, Not Speaking

People who suffer from too much 'stream of consciousness' might also be writing exactly how they speak. Yet in literature, it's important to distinguish between writing and speaking modes, because one is not the same as the other.

Listen to people talk – ideas might be on rapid-fire, while there's usually lots of 'erm' and 'yes, I know' repetitions from respondents. You might be a person noted for your verbal skill and repartee. Subjects in conversations zigzag back and forth as people take up and develop points said earlier. Voices will overlap. Silent participants can still be seen and their faces are indicating their levels of interest. Not much attention is paid to grammar. Sentences will be half-finished, with the hearer filling in details for themselves. Much will be conveyed non-verbally, through gestures and expressions. Close associates might almost speak in code because they automatically know the others' needs.

What's Wrong?

Surely it's natural to write in the same way as normal people speak? And it's easy for a great talker to do, bearing in mind their inherent ability to string words together in an effective way. But not all of this looks good in print. Why not? Because:

> You have to convey plot-related information. Pointless conversations, which show us nothing and describe no incidents, are going to clog up your story. They will take attention away from what the book is trying to say. Dialogue in a book should convey information about the characters or the plot.

> The reader can't see anything unless you tell them what's there. Referring to 'them', 'that one over there' or 'it' makes little sense if the reader hasn't been explicitly told who 'they' are or what 'it' is.

> If writing an autobiographical piece, the reader doesn't know you or any of the incidents you mention. Things should be explained in a coherent way.

> You might need to (artily) describe some of the non-verbal communication. Moods and silences … they all speak volumes, and writing ability is needed.

> We have to know who is talking and who is narrating, on occasions where it seems unclear.

> ➢ As readers, we have to grasp the point of a conversation early on.
> ➢ Without recognisable sentence structure in the narrative parts, it won't be publishable or easy to read.

While spelling, layout and consistent tones of voice don't matter in real-life conversations, they are crucial in making useful, publishable text.

Study Tips

Boundaries are blurred in email exchanges, which, unless strictly business, tend to approximate informal conversation. Your writing for readers should be alive like your emails, but with a higher level of formal correctness.

Grasp this point about writing and speaking modes by comparing dialogues and narrative passages from the same book.

Remember that recycling any true and naturalistic conversations will be far too drawn out and full of waffle for a short story. We'll get the picture after one or two 'I know, I know' interjections. There's a limit to the number of 'oh's you can use on the same page.

Better Starting Techniques

You might have a great story to tell. Unfortunately the first paragraph lets you down and the reader decides not to stay with it. This is one of the top reasons for rejections by publishers – the opening passages simply weren't grabbing them hard enough. Ah, you think. But my novel is five hundred pages – I need the time for expansion. Wrong – you don't have the time for expansion, because a busy reader isn't interested in the remaining four hundred and ninety nine pages if the first page hasn't told them it's worth hanging in there for the duration.

Your opening paragraph always sets the standard for what follows, and in the case of short fiction and poetry, the first line may be the only indicator that you're a proper writer who's in it for the long haul. So creaking starts, and lengthy preambles, will give the wrong impression even if your book or story is brilliant.

Effective starts are not impossible. You'll already know from the previous chapter that it's important to write your opening lines from a position of strength – waiting until you're further on in your script and confident about the direction it should take, waiting until the 'right' sentence suddenly occurs, even writing the start after you have finished the ending. You can also speed up your starts and have an engaged-sounding opener if you try some of the following:

> Begin on a line of dialogue – the reader wants to know who said it and why.
> Begin on an action or incident: a door slams, a car drives off, the burglar prises up the window.
> Begin halfway through a crisis. Your reader will want to know the outcome.
> Begin with a surprising announcement: your narrator says he's dead, the one who escaped, the person responsible for the issue in the book.
> Begin with a brief flashback before cutting to the present day.

Yes – it's a bit like the opening of a film. People are now so used to the jump-cut language of film scenes that they expect roughly the same to happen in popular fiction. Be prepared to rewrite your first paragraph more than once, in the light of what happens later in your story.

Exercise

Go to a bookshop or library, and look briefly at the opening paragraphs of books at random. Some of them will show openers based along the lines I have given above. If you find any alternatives, note them down for future reference. Now contrast these openers with famous novels from the past; Hardy, Dickens, the Brontes. Those old-fashioned slow starts were geared towards people who read novels during long evenings when there were no competing forms of entertainment.

Plagiarism

This is where someone else claims you have borrowed sections from their works and passed them off as your own. There are two types: intentional and unintentional. Sometimes, cynical literary chancers imagine that nobody will spot their wholesale liftings from other authors – they shove in whole paragraphs word for word, or insert large chunks of other people's research without attributing their sources and contacting any publishers for permission.

Younger writers in education might have come across papers and essays available on the Internet, ready to be downloaded at a price and passed off as your own work. In all these examples, the writers have committed plagiarism.

Unintentional plagiarism is more difficult to prove. Authors claim to be unaware that they've repeated another's work in their latest novel, or that they have no knowledge of the supposed source. 'It's all a big mistake' is the usual response. Despite the warning notices placed in libraries, clauses in contracts, and information packs issued to students, people still chance their arm as though it wasn't an offence. At the time of writing, there are three newsworthy cases in the broadsheets.

New writers might not be aware that it's important to attribute quotes, while inexperienced editors might miss the borrowings and copied paragraphs. One thing is certain – your book will be withdrawn from sale (and you can be dropped by your publisher) if you are proved to be a plagiarist. Editors take any accusations seriously and investigators will check your works. So don't get involved at any stage! Don't take paragraphs from another person's work, and always list your sources if you are quoting from a book.

Very short quotations are allowed for the purposes of criticism and review, and that's all. Otherwise, you need permissions from authors and their literary estates if you want to quote anything at length. Plagiarism can lead to court cases and lost reputations, so it's not a good way to become a writer. If you're the sort who sucks up influences like a Dyson on hyper-drive, ask a responsible person to check your manuscripts before you send them off.

Essential Things to Do

If borrowing a few quotes to place in the body of a fictional work – say, a novel where a character is always repeating items from a favourite authority – it's polite to attribute your borrowings on the acknowledgements page at the front of your book.

Non-fiction books should follow a recognised way of referencing other authors. A standard method is to place the name, book title, publisher, and date in brackets after any quotations. If you use the same book more than once, subsequent mentions inside your paragraphs can be followed by a brief form of the title instead of the whole sequence. Instead of 'William Anstruther's *Anecdotes of an Eighteenth Century Scottish Traveller*' every time, you can list 'Anstruther, *Anecdotes*' and the reader will know.

When seeking permission for long quotations taken from books in copyright, try the publishers first and they will forward any letters to the right person. Remember that most authors are only too happy to receive the free publicity!

Morality Tales

You already know about old fables and parables, where a moral message is given at the conclusion. Money is the root of all evil, good wins out in the end, the wily fox doesn't catch the little red hen; they're part of our cultural history. But nobody likes being preached-at in contemporary literature. Obvious morality messages not only spoil your tale by getting in the way – they make your characters appear two-dimensional. This is because rounded people are being cut down to fit one model, that of representing a few attitudes or vices for the sake of your moral point. The overall effect is both clumsy and old-fashioned, which is not something you should aspire to – particularly if there is a moral basis to your story!

Good writers know that any messages should be conveyed by stealth. This means revealing attitudes and beliefs gradually through the use of situations, dialogues, and character motivation. Never over-explain or spell it out, because readers are intelligent people and they can cope with sub-plots and hidden ideas. Some of our greatest writers have been campaigners and moralists of one kind or another; think of D.H. Lawrence arguing for honesty about sex in *Lady Chatterley's Lover* and elsewhere. The problem is, all of the big subjects have been done, and the time for didactic literature is long gone.

If you carry strong moral attitudes on the surface of your writing, it won't be in line with how current literature is read and experienced, unless you are writing for a clearly defined audience with (for example) the same religion as yourself. And the same applies to poets – unless you are writing comic verse like Hilaire Belloc's *Cautionary Tales*, your poem will paradoxically lose out if you end on a moralising tone. Why? Because a non-moralising poem will give a greater range of readers food for thought, including those who don't share the same opinions as the poet. You can view it as a poem; you can view it as a moral piece; either way, the audience is doubled and the publishing outlets are increased.

Looking Outside Yourself

The first section in this chapter dealt with the issue of personal therapy and creative writing, but there is an allied problem, which produces a similar outcome. Some new writers are so self-absorbed that they imagine anything written by themselves is a creative statement. Their small woes and sorrows are worthy of deep examination, their personalities are endlessly fascinating – and when they look in the bathroom mirror, they see a genius of the literary arts.

Believe me, nobody wants to know at length about your troubles with the world and how many people have conspired to give you grief over the years. They probably won't find your nice week in the Lake District very exciting. Family history is never a riveting subject for outsiders, unless you happen to be related to a person with sales potential – Dick

Turpin, for example, or Princess Anastasia. If a reader can't identify with your statements because they only refer to your own enclosed little world, you might fail in your job as a writer.

Moreover, self-absorption can appear unintentionally comic – and I'm sure you don't want readers laughing at you for the wrong reasons. George and Weedon Grossmith wrote a comic masterpiece when they created Mr. Pooter in *The Diary of a Nobody*; the whole point being that the self-important fusspot Pooter never realises just how banal and trivial his concerns are to the outside world.

Are Famous People Different?

If you read someone who is also a 'personality' – let's say, a travel-writer who presents a TV series – you will find that the work isn't really about the writer. It's about the experience he or she is having, and that celebrity writer will be doing all they can to make sure you share in the experience. You too will envisage the curious accommodation, the exotic nightlife and the many embarrassments of being abroad. And the writer will be using his or her position as leverage to enter into unusual buildings, forbidden corners, and situations, which bring you an interesting tale. Read the travel writings of Redmond O'Hanlon or Bill Bryson if you don't believe me. They are both larger than life personalities, yet we learn about the world through their experiences.

Songwriters often use their painful inner-feelings, but CDs sell because those same emotions are relevant to other people and expertly communicated in performance. Few of them just get up and do it – they have honed their stage personas and TV shticks over years of practice and rapport with their audiences. Moreover, celebrity presenters have teams of researchers and editors working behind the scenes. Often, somebody else has done the writing for them. It's no accident that celebrities have to hire ghost writers (actual word-loving writers with literary skill) when they compile their memoirs!

Caution – Ego In Transit

Remember, nobody can see the literature if your ego is blocking the way. It's fine to use your experience as subject matter, but it's essential to look outside of yourself. Navel-gazing ruminations and whimsical armchair musings often produce the worst kinds of amateur literature heard at readings, and it's best to kick the habit right now. Apart from telling the audience nothing of importance, it'll be impossible to publish later on! If this is you, stop before it's too late. Always consider the following:

- Why should anyone listen to me?
- Is this really just for my family and friends, not the wider world?
- What am I trying to tell the reader?
- Am I standing in the way of communication?
- Is this better off as diary material rather than written up as literature?
- If trading on my personality, am I sufficiently inclusive towards the world?
- If writing a self-absorbed work, is it sufficiently original and new?

It's very difficult to write about yourself without coming across as well worth avoiding on the street, as celebrity authors will often demonstrate without realising! If you've held a managerial post or worked alone for many years, seeing matters from another person's point of view may not come naturally on paper. But you have to stand in others' shoes if you want to be a writer.

An Example

A Heartbreaking Work of Staggering Genius by Dave Eggers (Picador, 2000) will show you one way of handling the difficult subject of 'yourself' and 'family history' while sounding like a contemporary author instead of a nineteenth century antiquarian.

> **Study Tip**
> If you're lucky enough to have lived an exotic or dangerous life, you can get away with it all... as long as every sentence doesn't begin with 'I'!

Conclusions

Your subject matter is a personal decision, but some things – like excessive introspection and too many streams of consciousness – will drive away readers unless your writing is handled carefully.

It pays to jettison out-of-date language if you are writing about 'now'.

Clichés and stereotypes are unoriginal, and they don't show you in a positive light. Most people can think of improvements and alternatives to them.

Don't pass off another's work as your own. It's not legal and your books or essays will be rendered worthless. If using quotes and examples, attribute them to their original authors.

Tutorial Section

Points for Discussion

1. What attracts you to a story?
2. Are there any circumstances where therapeutic writing is the same as creative writing?
3. Why are archaic words acceptable in a period-set story but not acceptable in poems?
4. Why are people so resistant to changing their work?

Practice Questions

1. It was on the fifth of August
   > The weather hot and fine
   Unto Brigg Fair I did repair
   > For love I was inclined.

   This charming folksong verse has several archaic features and a rhyme problem. Rewrite it in a contemporary way.

2. Take a famous Shakespearian speech (Hamlet's 'To be or not to be …' is a good one) and rewrite it using a contemporary situation and style.
3. Which popular clichés do you come across every day?
4. Collect any unusual family sayings or phrases, which could prove useful to you as a writer.
5. Devise a celebrity character and write a 'stream of consciousness' page as that person.
6. Check up the current regulations on copyright. This will give you the full information on what you can and can't use. Luckily, it's not as restrictive as it sounds. Write down what is allowable and keep it in your files.

Beat the Block

You've learnt about some techniques, and discovered how to overcome the most common problems which new writers face. But what about the problems which you haven't created for yourself, and those which seem inevitable? In this chapter you'll find out more about the dreaded 'writer's block' and what to do if it strikes. Read on to discover some useful strategies for giving the block a good kick out of your system.

The Block

What is Writer's Block? Does It Exist?

Horror stories abound. The famous novelist who wrote nothing for years. The poet who never got beyond one award-winning poem. Something of the sort has happened to the well-known literary greats. You might be surprised to discover that Jane Austen went for a period of ten years writing nothing, after being forced to leave her favourite home by parents who desired town life in Bath. And the poet WS Graham had a fifteen-year silence between collections.

No doubt about it, writers can seize up for great periods of time. In fact, the actuality is so common that it's time people stopped thinking of it as a problem. Having the block is what happens when you've run out of material, or when you sit down to work but you can't think of anything. And the more you think about it, the worse it gets. The worse it gets, the less you write, and the more worried you become. It's a vicious circle.

Journalists, on the other hand, don't believe in writer's block. They have to write every day at work whether they feel like it or not, otherwise the editor would sack them. Consequently, when a journalist becomes a novelist, they hardly ever have problems with writer's block. For them, writers who complain of being blocked are simply whingeing.

If you read a collection of writers' quotes, like *Advice to Writers* (ed. Jon Winokur, Pavilion Books, 2000) you will find conflicting and contradictory opinions on whether it exists. Joyce Carol Oates maintains that it doesn't, Toni Morrison says that it does. But both concede that the solution is only a matter of time; work has stopped because you're not ready for it yet. Later, you will be. Is the glass half empty or half full? You decide.

See things in perspective

If you're a starter, it's unlikely you will be troubled with the block. Not writing for a week while you deal with the kitchen fitters isn't the same as writer's block. Neither is being too miserable to write because an aunt has died. These are 'life events'. Not writing because you are too lazy to get up earlier on Sundays…that's not writer's block neither.

If you aren't writing for whatever reason, see it in perspective. Are you naturally a boom and bust writer, having long gaps between stories and poems? Don't worry – another work is probably trying to unfold in your imagination, only it's not made contact with your brain yet.

Have you just completed a massive document at work, led a successful enterprise, or written a novel in six weeks? It's likely your mind is saying 'stop, for heaven's sake'. So there won't be any poems for a while, then.

And there won't be many works if you're stressed, ill, taking exams, or otherwise unable to sit down with a pen. None of these are writer's block either. Or maybe you just can't be bothered? Writer's block is not an excuse for doing nothing.

Learn to recognise the 'pain barrier'. This is when you're busy writing a substantial work, and it suddenly feels both pointless and a burden, stretching ahead for months. Everything becomes an uphill struggle, your writing seems poor, and you wonder why you ever started. Many experienced writers recognise this feeling, and it often hits a third to halfway through the projected work. It's very similar to the athlete's pain barrier, and all you should do is… carry on.

Beyond the halfway mark, you will see that more lies written than unwritten. That's when the pain barrier tends to lift, so don't mistake it for a block.

If you think you have writer's block

- ➢ Accept the fact. Then get on with something else – if you can go away for a few days, plan a break and take it. A short holiday is often enough to shift a block.
- ➢ By dismissing the block's right to rule your life, you diminish its power.
- ➢ Tell people honestly that you're not writing just now. Pretending you're still active will make you feel like a fraud, and that'll make the blockage worse.
- ➢ If you pretend to be writing when you're not, people won't believe you in the future.
- ➢ Never blame your family, friends, or workmates. It probably isn't them anyway.
- ➢ Clear away the half-finished works you're stuck on, and forget them for now.

Some Solutions

Are you combining writing with another art, such as drama or painting? It's likely you're not meant to do both at the same time. For some people, writing originates from the same place as their complementary art, and one is 'off' when the other is 'on'.

Relaxation, inner serenity, self-esteem and freedom of expression can have an impact on your ability to write. Look at any issues you might have relating to these. Low self-esteem and an associated feeling of 'it's just no use' is unlikely to result in a masterpiece.

Too much head-work? Country walking, games and play, sports, retail therapy, cooking, clubbing. … just do it.

Maybe the work is the problem, not you. The plot isn't interesting, the poem is dull, you don't like any of your characters. Maybe this project isn't so good. Shelve it.

Are you laying down enough plans for your work? Writers can easily run out of steam because they have insufficient idea of what's coming next. If you have an outline for your chapter, and you know where your characters are going, a block is unlikely to happen.

Read aspirational books which feed the imagination and create a feel-good factor. Some of the creative manuals issued by American publishers are particularly good; Julia Cameron's *The Artist's Way* (Pan, 1995) is recommended.

Some people enjoy small rituals which lead naturally into writing – always sharpening their pencils before they start, keeping talismans and symbols on their desks, etc. If this is you, establish a positive routine and stick to it; especially while you're engaged on the particularly problematic areas of the work.

Change the time of day when you normally start writing. H.G. Wells recommended taking the blocked work by surprise like this.

Try a new day job in case too much complacent routine is dulling your senses. If you're free to write whenever you choose, take a walk around a run-down business district and think of the sorry people in there who'd rather be out where you are. Then get back to the desk…

And here's what not to do. Drink or drugs are not the solution to writer's block, as various dead authors have found out to their cost. Bingeing and illegal stimulants will make you so incompetent that you'll never write anything decent again. Just say no.

Exercises to Keep You Going

So the block has struck, and you find it difficult to write the next chapter of your novel. You've had a holiday, there's nothing fundamentally wrong… but still it doesn't work. You need some or all of the following, if you are going to break out of the cycle. Remember that any writing is better than no writing.

Take a notebook line and start there; revise old work which you left a long time ago. Returning to a different stage in your writing will often shake off a temporary blockage.

If you tend to seize up completely when you can't think of the right word, do what Jack Kerouac did; when stuck mid-flight, he would put a nonsense phrase like 'blahblahblah', until ready to return to the phrase after the next part has flowed naturally.

Sign up for the nearest workshop. Don't worry if the result is forced and mechanical or the tutor is useless. You have written something.

> Your old photograph albums: what happened to those characters after the picture was taken?
> Rewrite a poem into a piece of descriptive prose, or vice versa.
> Cut out sentences from newspapers, and note down random lines from a range of books. Next, fit these assorted lines together. Sometimes a surreal narrative develops.
> Ask someone in your house to give you five separate words, which must be fitted into a one-page short story.
> Postcard Epics: try to reduce the plot of a famous book into the space allowed on a postcard.
> Proverbs and sayings: take a well-known fable, proverb, or saying, and devise a new story for how that saying came about.
> Think of your writer heroes. How would they climb out of a block?
> Open a book at random and take the first line you see as a starting point.
> Look at crossword clues and see if you can spot a narrative happening between various points in the text. Then use these lines to construct a poem.
> Go outside and use the public places exercise mentioned in Chapter 3. So many blocks result because the writer has no input. Think of the sausage machine... you'll have no sausages if there's no meat in the grinder.

Most of the above suggestions have been used at some point by writers – yes, they really work; even the surreal random sentences one. In Australia during the 1940s, two poets caused a notorious literary scandal by writing a whole collection using that method.

Writer's block can be an awkward presence in a writer's life. But it needn't be something to fear. Only a minority of writers suffer the deep psychological versions which result in a need for therapy or medication. The rest of us have simply run out of fresh material for a while. If you're not under deadline to produce a book by the fifteenth of next month, you have little to fear and nothing to worry about.

Conclusions

You've discovered what 'writer's block' is – but that some believe it doesn't exist at all.

You've discovered lots of solutions to get you starting again, should you feel you've run out of fresh writing material.

You've hopefully realized never to let 'writer's block' become a serious issue – you don't want to be a has-been or, worse, a never-was!

Tutorial Section

Points for Discussion

1. Do you believe there is such a thing as 'writer's block'? Which side are you on?
2. Do you think most people suffer from 'writer's block' in terms of thinking up material, or in terms of transforming their vision into words?
3. How would you deal with a long silence in your writing?

Practice Questions

1. If you have suffered from writer's block in the past, identify the causes.
2. Research authors on the Internet and see what small rituals they have used to lead them naturally into writing.
3. A new perspective can offer restore creativity. Try some lateral thinking:

   Recall your favourite television shows through the years. Relating your answers to just the titles of the programmes, imagine what these shows could have been about. For example: if *Only Fools and Horses* was about two academically-challenged brothers aspiring to be jockeys.

7

Dealing with Rejection and General Troubleshooting

One Minute Overview

Rejection is one event that commonly precedes an episode of writer's block. This chapter examines the many reasons that publishing houses and editors may have for rejecting your work, and advises you on why you should continue submitting even if you have received a rejection note – or several. Is the lack of encouragement a little closer to home though? We focus here also on the reasons why your friends or family may not support you in your aims as a writer, and how you can deal with this situation. Finally, there's an examination of the other most common concerns expressed by new writers.

Handling Rejection

Rejection slips happen to every author of every standard, so it's wise to expect some. Even if your work is good, not everyone will like it. Yes, you too will get the thick envelope – your prized script – back on your table at home. But constant rejection can leave new authors thinking 'why bother', and it becomes harder to retain interest levels and motivation. The resulting negativity can cause writer's block, or long silences between works – times when an author still wants to write, but nothing happens apart from the usual rejection slips. Why continue at all? Why put yourself through more of the same? Plenty of people give up writing at this point.

By the end of this handbook you should be considering some markets and trying a submission. It helps, therefore, if you know more about why rejections happen and what you can do about them. Let the following information lift the lid on the nature of an editor's rejection note.

Why Editors Reject

Here are some reasons why editors reject poetry and short fiction on the literary magazines circuit:

- ➢ Recent change of editorship – they have new preferences.
- ➢ They run on a narrow range of contributors and you didn't know.
- ➢ Too many submissions – turning away the excess numbers regardless of quality.
- ➢ Office power politics – the assistant rejected it without showing the main editor.
- ➢ It's a themed issue and your work doesn't fit the theme.
- ➢ You really did send in some bad ones.
- ➢ You just missed the deadline for the next issue and they don't save work.
- ➢ The money's run out – no magazines for the rest of the year.
- ➢ An opinionated editor and they don't agree with your stance.
- ➢ An editorial board which can't make a clear decision, so they reject it.
- ➢ Your best poem doesn't fit the space available.
- ➢ Your poems are good but they can't understand some of the lines.

As you can see, only one of the above reasons is to do with the quality of the work you sent in! Bigger publishers will use other reasons – the main ones being a) whether your work will sell, and b) whether the editor is as passionate about the story as you are. They won't admit it, but a great deal of acceptances are down to whether an editor just likes it or not, once it is clear that your writing is up to scratch in the first place.

The brief rejection note, then, isn't often saying 'your work is terrible'. It's more likely to be saying 'I'm an overworked editor who hasn't got the time or the room right now'. It's painful to see your work when it lands again on the doormat, but if you think of it as returned rather than rejected, this helps to put it in perspective. Editors' tastes vary, and the same piece may be accepted by someone who has opposite tastes to the one you tried before.

Assuming that there's nothing wrong with your piece – it's written to the best of your ability, it's double-spaced and page perfect – what can you do about this dismal situation?

Don't Give Up

When the going gets tough, the tough simply buy more stamps and envelopes. Rather than give yourself anxiety over a returned piece of work, print out a fresh copy and send it to the next journal on your list. It's not unusual for a book script to find a home after twenty or thirty publishers have been approached. A poem could be on the road for a couple of years before an editor says yes.

Learn to accept that your life as a writer will involve a lot of rejection notes, and laugh about it. Florid or uncomprehending replies can be pinned to the wall for darts practice, or used to line the hamster's cage. Pull the rejection note from its envelope, and put it immediately in the bin. The editor doesn't know you, and you don't deserve to be upset or annoyed. They have to read some appalling scripts, and sometimes (on a bad day) anything is enough to set them off.

Useful replies – critical points about your work, friendly comments from the editor –should be saved in your cuttings book. If it seems that the editor likes your work, try them again in a few months' time. It will help your confidence to read the number of positive responses you can attract, even if the work itself has been returned.

Keep sending other work out while you are waiting for the results on your main project. That way your hopes don't solely rest on the outcome of one submission.

There is an unseen benefit to posting out your work – you are circulating as a writer, and your name is on people's desks. Skilled editors notice good new writers, even if the first few submissions have to be rejected.

Finally

Never (and I mean never) write back to an editor complaining about the rejection. Never harass an editor in any way. It will only prejudice them against your future work.

The *other* 'never' is… never send out a first draft, or anything with bad spelling and poor grammar. The editor will know that it's undeveloped, while inaccuracies will annoy them terribly. Editors are fine-tuned when it comes to typos and mistakes, because they see so many scripts. And many of them will have backgrounds in journalism and teaching.

Troubleshooting

Sixteen common concerns expressed by new writers

While on the subject of blocks, obstructions, and rejection, it's a good idea to look at some of the other issues you might encounter as a writer. The following questions are among the commonest worries I hear from students at all stages of development. Maybe one of these generic replies will solve a problem for you, or end those minor niggles which prevent you from feeling in control.

I don't know any writers or anyone like that

The quickest way is to join a local class or group, even if you don't need tuition. And there's virtually a year-round programme of literary festivals in Britain now, with heavyweight fests alternating with small countryside events in attractive locations. There's something to suit everyone, and they're a great place for meeting other writers. Creative people like to associate with those who share the same outlook, and sociability is important if you're aiming at networking so that you can be recognised in future. If your town runs an arts festival, you could join the volunteers who support the administrative team.

I'd like some hot-housing please – but I don't like classroom situations

Contact the Arvon Foundation (see bibliography) for their yearly programme. Loads of help, and all the time you need. Many writers benefit from their residential weeks, and there are subsidised places for those on low incomes. Some regional arts organisations operate mentoring schemes – contact your regional arts officers for the latest details. At the time of writing, the concept of 'mentoring' in the arts is on the rise, where an experienced writer offers one-to-one tuition for a limited period. Other arts bodies may hold weekends in residential colleges, or special networking days and conferences, where you can pick up valuable advice and short cuts. Contact your Arts Council branch and outline what it is exactly you want.

My family/colleagues/friends are not supportive

This is a frequent problem. Yet opinions change as soon as publication happens... now isn't that curious? Any possibility of earnings should keep them quiet. In the meantime:

➢ Don't lay yourself open to damaging opinions if you're a sensitive type or subjected to discouragement. Instead, say as little as possible about your writing until some tangible result has occurred: a good story, a selection of poems, an acceptance note, a gig.

➢ Don't leave your work lying around – it's an open invitation for them to scoff at your early stuff.

➢ Cafés and libraries are great places to write in. So are store-rooms, cars, and public parks. You may have a well-intentioned boss who'll let you use the office computer at lunchtime, or a friend may let you use their address for submissions.

> ➢ Join a group of local writers, or a reader's group; somewhere you can share a passion for literature.
> ➢ There are online resources and publishing outlets too; try some of those mentioned in the bibliography.

Unsupportive families fear three things: time spent away from serving them, a mysterious 'change' in the person who previously wasn't a writer, and mere fantasising that results in nothing which they value. Listen out for words like 'scribblings', 'impractical', 'dreaming' and the steadfast refusal to believe that you can do it. This will show you their attitude even if nothing is made absolute. Two more concerns they might have: they'll fear you giving up your job (there goes the new freezer and the second car) or they'll think it's a passing fad, which will eat up your resources ('it was archery and butterfly collecting last year'). It's unlikely you will change any of their opinions in the short term.

In extreme cases, it might be better for you to find a whole new set of friends, or at least part company with those who are holding you back. Approaching the matter of what they fear about your writing might open a way forward. Parents can be alarmed to discover that their sweet bouncing baby has turned into a zombie-death-gothic-horror writer, and unfortunately families thrive on pigeon-holing their members in the belief that no-one grows or changes. Close friends are alarmed to discover there's more to you than they thought. Try to understand their point of view occasionally!

I can never think of titles

Your notebook should be useful here. If eye-catching titles are not your strong point, use a line from within the work or a quotation from another source that has relevance to your work. It's possible to use numbers or the date of composition. Borrow associative titles from other arts or sciences; pictures, chemistry and music have all been raided by writers in search of good phrases. The Bible is a treasury of effective titles. Remember that there's no copyright in titles, so it's quite all right to borrow phrases providing no confusion will arise – for example, it would be foolish to write a novel entitled *The Grapes of Wrath* or *Midnight's Children*. Keep collecting good phrases in your notebook for use as suitable titles – even when you have no specific book in mind.

I want to use a pen name. How do I make sure the payments can be cashed by me?

Publishers are used to this one, because they deal with hundreds of writers whose real names are different to those on their book jackets. All you have to do is this. On your title sheet below the book title, put your pen name: let's say *Torrid Nights*, by Desiree Devereaux. In the bottom right hand corner where the author's address usually goes, put your real name. The editorial staff will know they should be paying Mabel Sprocket, not Desiree. You can always provide both names on your covering letter too – naming the pen name along with your title, while signing the letter with your real name. Don't forget that many married women use a previous surname, and a common ploy involves using an ancestral name, when your own isn't so interesting.

I've heard that good ideas can be stolen from unknown writers by editors or production staff. How can I prevent this happening?

Firstly, you have to realise that other people can have similar ideas to you. It isn't unusual for a script to arrive at the same time as another one, using exactly the same plot derived from similar sources. This situation has always existed. Before 1914, the poet Rupert Brooke sent a one-act shocker in to a prominent theatrical impresario. She replied that it was the sixth play she had received on the same subject. A British playwriting competition in 2006 hauled in over two thousand entries, with over three hundred of these set in gyms and health clubs.

It's not unusual for two biographers to be at work on the same subject for different publishers at the same time, or for researchers, entirely unknown to each other, to write very similar articles. Ideas arriving through shared cultural sources – newspapers, television, and other books – are accessible to anyone, and other writers will find the same sources as you. What's worse is that there's no copyright on ideas. People are not stealing your work, and there's no conspiracy – it's just that people think like other people, and we all respond to the same stimuli.

If you're worried about protecting your copyright against theft, the following old trick might help. When you send your submission, send a duplicate package to yourself, using registered post or recorded delivery, or any other method involving signatures and serial numbers. Leave this package unopened in a safe place, with the postmark and stickers untouched. If you suspect your work has been recycled under another name, you have the dated proof of your story being ready beforehand.

People laugh in the wrong places, or when it's not funny

You are reading your works to the wrong audience. Otherwise, you could be taking yourself too seriously in your writing, so that people find you unintentionally comic. Are you merely exhibiting common faults, which are easily corrected, like: bombast, poor rhyming, bathos, wooden or unnatural dialogue? Are there unconscious ironies in your work which you haven't spotted yet? A bit of analysis will pay off. Get an honest opinion from a straight-talking critic, and follow their advice. Alternatively, you could capitalise on the funny tendency and turn it to a style advantage, becoming conscious of the effect you are creating. Many comedians have worked out of this dilemma and gone on to enjoy successful creative careers.

I write too much – it's all formless slabs

This is a good sign, because it means you're an energetic and involved writer with more material than you can cope with. After a writing session, begin a second draft, which is far shorter, picking out the essentials of the matter and the most striking sentences. But don't throw away your first draft, because it will contain other ideas for the future. Is your work better off as a short story or an article? Most people end up revising down (cutting things out) rather than stretching up (adding bits on). Therefore, most people have to work with formless slabs rather than pleasant neat paragraphs saying exactly what they wanted. You're not alone!

If you are a poet, remember that editors don't have any space for epics, and you will increase your chances of rejection by sending out a poem which prints longer than two A5-sized pages. It's possible that a long or directionless piece is two or more separate ones mixed up together, so always leave your work and return to it at a later date – at which point, the themes will be more apparent.

Do I need to put © after my name to claim copyright on my work?

No. Copyright is automatically yours once the work is written down. It can't be transferred to a third party or stolen from you, although you can sell on various rights if you're daft enough. What's more, copyright on published work is still yours until 70 years after your death. Isn't that nice to know? You'll see © listed on the frontispiece of books, but if you send out your scripts plastered with ©, it will say 'amateur' and 'first timer' to an editor at the receiving end.

I'm too scared to write in case it's bad

Starting is always an issue, particularly if you have a time-consuming project in mind. Fool yourself into starting by writing a short prologue first, or make character notes until you are engrossed in how these people will turn out. Carry a few lines around in your head all day, or have a sentence or two folded up in your purse. Imagine what your characters might be doing – even if it's unrelated to the story you intend – and write that down instead.

Sometimes it's being at the start which is the problem and not the actual writing; so begin at the most exciting part of your narrative and work backwards. Banish all thoughts of whether it is 'bad' until you are at least two chapters in. Then reconsider. Is there enough mileage in the story, and are you prepared to carry on?

What do they mean by 'house style'?

These are features peculiar to individual journals or publishing departments; unusual fonts or layouts, specific ways of referencing quotations, particular tones of voice required, etc. A house style could involve poems where every line has to begin with a capital letter, or where no story should be longer than two thousand words. You can save yourself a lot of hassle by requesting any house style requirements from a magazine editor before you write for them. Enclose a self-addressed envelope, and you'll get a sheet of guidelines from an editor who already knows that you're taking some trouble to write what they need.

I'm afraid of success – being known and recognised, that kind of thing

In all honesty, why are you in the business of writing if the thought of being successful puts you off? In most cases, writers' lives don't change much once they have crossed over from unpublished to published. Most writers are never asked to perform at major festivals, most do not sign lucrative book deals and move to a warmer climate. If the thought of success is a major issue, there is no need to publish. Plenty of people out there who will take your place on the bookshelves!

Will I need an agent?

No, not until you are publishing and you have a track record. An agent is primarily for novelists – if you become a poet, freelance journalist or short story writer, you can dispense with the services of an agent. Agents are looking for profit – if your work is not commercial or mainstream, you are wasting your time forwarding your work to an agent first.

I've sent out hundreds of submissions and they've all been rejected

If you are targeting the right outlets, maybe it's time to face the truth. Are you practised enough? The more you send out, the greater the potential acceptance rate. Setting yourself a time limit may help; three or four years is sensible. If you've had no acceptances – not even from a very modest outlet – consider another type of writing or even a different art form altogether. Don't spend your life under an illusion, and it's best not to compromise a good job or career in the pursuit of an unobtainable artistic goal. Writing is competitive when it comes to the selling end. If you're a very young writer it may be a result of all-round inexperience…. in which case, you don't have much to worry about.

They say I'm derivative

Ask your critics to expand – it's not enough for them to say that you sound like someone else without them specifying who exactly it is. Certain contemporary styles are widespread anyway and these won't prevent you from being published. The one to avoid is: sounding exactly like an author who has a very distinctive style. In short, belonging to a style sub-group or genre is acceptable, but close copying of one particular author isn't. Meanwhile, if you are a beginner, don't worry if your work sounds like someone else's or the last thing you read. It's a time-honoured way of learning, as described earlier.

When I look at the photos on book jackets, they're all 20-something glamour people. What chance have I got?

The same chance as everyone else of course! The media will always have an eye for youth and glamour, which is good news for any ex-high school queens and surfer dudes planning a first novel during their gap year. But look at it from the editor's point of view – he or she will have no idea of your age or appearance or income levels at the point when you submit your manuscript…. unless you've told them. Some inexperienced writers enclose their age in brackets along with their signature on the covering letter, which is something you should never do. If you have a very dated name which positively screams 'born in 1930', why not change it? Meanwhile, the real publishing industry (not the media circus) is more than happy to take a risk on authors over the age of 50. They still select on the basis of merit and/ or commercial potential, despite what the media would have us believe. There's at least one major prize (the Sagittarius), which is awarded to authors over 60. Novelist Mary Wesley and poet Ida Affleck Graves were both over 70 when their first successful books appeared. Need I go on?

Conclusions

Writers of all backgrounds experience a range of issues, from poor attempts at titles to partners who actively get in the way and try to prevent them from writing. End isolation by sharing your works with like-minded people and building up alternative support networks.

Tutorial Section

Points for Discussion

1. What reasons may people have for not supporting a writer in their aims? How can you deal with this situation?
2. What reasons may editors have for rejecting people's work? Why should you continue submitting your work even if you have received rejections?
3. Do you think authors have a duty to adopt a style that makes them sound different from already published pieces?
4. What do you think is the best way for somebody interested in writing to meet fellow people in the field?

Practice Questions

1. Collect a range of books and periodicals together and work out whether any of them have followed a 'house style'.
2. How would you deal with the following situations?
   a) Two separate magazines have chosen the same poem/short article.
   b) An editor wants your piece, but you have to alter one character and cut out some images which you really laboured over.
   c) An editor returns your piece, enclosing a note which seriously misinterprets your work and insults your ability to write.
3. Do an Internet search for works in the arts or sciences, for example, famous photographs, sculptures, paintings or pieces of music, and create a list of those phrases that would be particularly good as book titles.
4. Recall mention of the British playwriting competition with over three hundred entries set in either a gym or a health club? Think of five locations which are less likely to have featured in the submissions.

This chapter is mercifully short, and I hope I haven't put you off writing. Next, we turn to the two big issues facing new writers who've made some progress and want to go further. These are: how to maximise your chances of being published, and how to join with other people and use your literary interests in a practical way.

8

Towards Publication

It's wonderful to see your work in print, and for many beginners having a book on the shelf is their ultimate aim. But getting it there is often a long journey down a narrow road strewn with heavy boulders. Writers can worry about making the wrong moves and putting the wrong details in their submissions, and it's fair to say that many rejections occur because the new writer hasn't yet understood the 'entry procedure'. This chapter will remove some of the mysteries about how to submit your work, and provide information about some useful stops on that difficult road. You'll learn about some of the formalities too: while covering letters and a synopsis might seem inessential at the moment, knowledge of these little extras can help smooth the way ahead, giving a professional look to your work.

Studying the Market

While working through this book, I hope you've used the suggested exercises to complete some literature of your own. In fact, if you haven't got a drawer full of half-finished items and miscellaneous writings by now, you're not nearly enthusiastic enough to make a convincing stab at authorship! So before considering the publications market, it helps if you are already the author of several short stories, nearing the end of at least twenty poems, or more than halfway towards finishing a novel. More than ever, publishers want work that is ready, not works in need of extensive revision.

If you are clear about your market, this section might be less important for you, although it's worth checking to make sure you are on the right lines. You might be the only person you know who is a writer, but authorship is the ambition of millions – and many of them will be submitting to the same publishers as you!

Where Does My Work Belong?

Firstly, assess the range of subjects you write about, and your preferred style – you might have more than one. Are your best pieces domestic in their contents, or difficult and literary, or within a specific genre, like sci-fi or crime? Is the language highly wrought and poetic, or plain and clear? Are you a storyteller, or a revealer of truths about mankind?

Having decided the overall tone of voice and subject range in your best work, you need to match it up with the range of outlets available. If you have the *Handbook* or the *Yearbook*, you will see subject listings, which conveniently split the publishers into their respective genres and what they publish. Look these up now, and familiarise yourself with the names.

Unfortunately, it isn't enough to just fire off your works to the given addresses. You need to have an in-depth knowledge of some of these outlets before submitting your works to them for consideration. Every day, countless publishers are deluged with work that simply doesn't fit their scheme of things. Therefore, you can stay one step ahead by remembering this sentence: know your outlets first.

Now try the following

Spend an hour in the library examining the books which are most like the type of work you are writing. Note down the publishers' names and addresses, and check to make sure that they still exist.

Choose a large chain bookstore – the sort which encourages browsers with armchairs and coffee bars – and examine the section which best suits your aims. Here you will find the latest publishers and new imprints from the conglomerates. Look at the styles being printed right now – are you happy with these, or is your work better off elsewhere?

Carry out the same examination of the magazine racks. Do you know which periodicals take work like yours, and are you a regular subscriber? If you are not buying any relevant magazines or journals, your knowledge of those outlets is probably too limited. An accurate picture of what the editors want can only be built up over a number of months. 'Cosy' magazines occasionally throw in a controversial article; left-wing outlets might occasionally present an opposing viewpoint. But you need to know when, where, and which editorial person is in charge.

Poetry and literary journals are often run by subscription only, and you might not find them in a bookshop. As the subscriptions largely fund the publishing, these literary outlets can't survive without reader/writer support, and you will be doing your bit for the survival of publishing by taking out a subscription. Among the names to look out for are: *The Rialto, Magma, The Reader, Smiths Knoll, Acumen, and Poetry Wales.*

Write to some of their addresses (*Handbook/Yearbook*) and ask for a subscription form, enclosing a self-addressed envelope. It's possible to purchase a couple of back issues if you can't afford or don't want to take out a regular subscription. Some have websites, as do the quality small presses who publish poetry. If you don't have the handbooks yet, write to the Poetry Library at the South Bank Centre in London (see bibliography). Enclose a self-addressed envelope and tell them you want the current list of magazines.

Big Press, Small Press

By now you will have noticed the two-tier system in British publishing. In one corner we have the major players: names like Harper Collins, Penguin, Faber, and Macmillan will be already familiar to you – big budgets, worldwide distribution, takeovers and deals, sub-divisions, imprints, and as many accountants as editors.

In the opposite corner we have small presses and mid-sized independents, usually owner-managed and dealing in shorter print-runs, niche marketing, and direct relations between the author and production side. Some are very small indeed, for example, a poet running a list of booklets on behalf of writer colleagues. Among the names you might find are: *Shoestring, Redbeck, SmithDoorstop, Flambard, and Seren.*

But small doesn't mean minor or poorly produced. Some of them are responsible for introducing future bestsellers and prizewinning works: Tindal Street Press scored a notable hit with *Astonishing Splashes of Colour* a few years ago. And many of them receive grants from the *Arts Council* or their equivalents, guaranteeing a good standard of production.

As a new author, your best chances of publication will arise through the small press route, particularly if you are a poet or short story writer. Therefore, become familiar with the small press world as it applies to you, and build up a track record there or in the small magazines before approaching mainstream publishers. Most of the poets on the Faber and Picador lists have begun this way, appearing in literary quarterlies and small magazines first.

Remember that mass market publishing responds to fashionable trends. At the time of writing, 'chick lit' is past its sell-by date, and 'crossover fiction', which suits both children and adults, is still riding high. You can improve your chances of acceptance by being close to the start of a commercial trend rather than following in its wake – something determined by your knowledge of the current publishing scene.

You can of course write exactly what you want and still become published, but it helps if you fit one of the recognised genres. In commercial fiction, a work which can't be placed with a relevant editor will probably be rejected – not because it is bad, but because it doesn't fit.

Take Action

Now that you have some insight into who publishes what, select your best short works – either stand-alone prose or several poems, and print them out using the guidelines supplied in the next paragraphs. By the end of this chapter you will be encouraged to make a first submission.

Submitting Your Work

The biggest problem editors face is the massive number of submissions they receive. The inside of an editor's office is a scary place to be when mis-spelt items jostle for attention with fifty-page verse autobiographies accompanied by handwritten notes in green ink. Before you submit any work, it greatly helps your case if the script looks professional from the outset. Therefore: banish any signs of eccentricity in your presentation.

> ➤ Use only black ink, unlined A4 paper, and clear typefaces like Arial, Times, Palatino.
> ➤ Leave good margins – editors often make notes in these.
> ➤ Enclose a contents list, unless you have a really good reason for not doing so.
> ➤ Do not send doodles, illustrations, or drawings along with your text. It doesn't make you look creative, original, or engaging; it looks disturbed.
> ➤ Attention-seeking moves like photographs, bribes, and presents, will cause laughter in the office.
> ➤ Think: clear, communicative, and businesslike.
> ➤ Include your address on the title page, and on the reverse of the last sheet.
> ➤ Avoid using staples or metal binders, pins and paperclips etc; editors prefer a pack of numbered loose sheets secured with an elastic band. Don't staple chapters together.
> ➤ Always enclose return postage, either a large self-addressed envelope, or addressed sticky labels and stamps if you are sending your piece in a re-usable Jiffy bag.

An editor will always want prose in double-spaced formatting, with numbered pages and text on one side of the paper only. Any failure to provide this and the editor will assume you're not a serious writer. I realise that some of this sounds rule-ridden and harsh, but these are the ways editors work. Unreadable printing, no margins, and messy pages are simply not going to be acceptable.

For novelists, the standard submissions package is as follows: the first three chapters, a synopsis, and a covering letter. The synopsis is far more important than it seems, because it shows you have thought about the overall direction of your novel and that most of it is completed even if your chapters after number five are still in draft form.

What Is A Synopsis?

A synopsis is a potted version of your plot, lasting about two pages. It should be written in the present tense if possible, outlining what happens from stage to stage in your narrative. You don't need complicated character descriptions or fleshed-out settings in this document; instead, put simply and baldly what happens from chapters one to three, four to six, and so on, divided into logical paragraphs.

You might be a writer who changes the scenario constantly, and yet you are required to tie yourself to this annoying synopsis thing before your novel is complete. Don't worry; most editors know that novels often change, and what they are looking for is the indication that you can follow through. They need proof that you have some progress in mind and a workable outcome for your story.

Synopsis practice can be obtained by summarising a famous novel or a book you have recently read. You might be a first time novelist, but a good synopsis written by an expert will gain the interest of an editor and they'll be tempted to read on. Think of a synopsis as a calling card or an advertisement for your work – include the striking incidents, the twists and turns.

The Covering Letter

This is your other important submissions document. In most cases, short is best. Follow the usual letters procedure with your address, telephone number or other contact details at the top right hand corner, and concluding the letter with 'yours sincerely'. Keep it simple, and no longer than a couple of paragraphs. If you have been published anywhere recently, let them know, because it helps if they can see you've had some experience. If you're a complete novice, don't tell them.

Here is an example of a typical covering letter text:

Dear Michael Trudger,

I'm enclosing a submission for Iron Bedsteads and a stamped return envelope. I'm not currently a subscriber to your magazine, but I have the previous five copies and I was interested in the themes for your forthcoming issues. I won the Littleborough Open Poetry Competition in 2005, and since then I've been working towards a first collection.

Yours sincerely,
Cindy Haystack.

The above letter shows the editor that Cindy is busy as a poet, not just a one-timer who might never write again. While she isn't a subscriber to this particular magazine yet, she has taken the trouble to read some back numbers and she's aware that *Iron Bedsteads* runs a theme for each edition. Her work might be rejected, but the editor can at least expect relevant poems, and he knows she is an engaged writer who has made an effort.

As with everything in publishing, there's a covering letter no-no for new writers – and it's this:

Don't opinionate or justify your works. It really will put the editors off.

In other words, let the work speak for itself. Your writing in the book should be what amazes and astounds, not the self-justifying statements you have sent alongside it. Your reasons for writing might be important, but the editor who receives a tirade or a screed will assume that the writer is an amateur or too difficult to deal with.

Study Tip

Keeping a template covering letter in your files will sort out those 'I don't know what to put' worries when you're packaging up a submission at short notice. Compile a model letter and leave a blank for the title of your work.

Trying an Agent

Novelists might be wondering whether an agent is a better option than submitting direct to a publisher, yet the position of many agents nowadays is little better than that experienced by publishers many years ago – they are receiving far more scripts than they used to, and first time novelists, with their unknown capabilities and low earning potential, are not a priority.

An agent is a middle-man or woman who approaches publishers on your behalf, negotiates a deal, and takes a percentage of the sales (currently 15%) as their fee. You will find them listed in the *Yearbook* or *Handbook*, along with their specialisms and preferences. With an agent you will have better deals and a career, and so it's important for a novelist or playwright to have one. But don't stunt your career by worrying whether you will have an agent or not; small publishers take work direct, and you can attract an agent through having a track record elsewhere. If you attend a literary event and someone calling themselves an agent has a conversation with you, take their business card and check them up in the appropriate listings.

If you have the budget for it, try a script assessment service. Some of them have links with agencies, and they often advertise in places like *Writing Magazine*. As with practically all assessment and editorial services, they can't offer it for free; but you will obtain an impartial and professional report.

Whether you are submitting to an agent or a publisher first, the format is the same:

> ➢ Check to make sure your work is relevant.
> ➢ Print out a clean synopsis, first three chapters and covering letter.
> ➢ Have a title page, also giving your name and address near the bottom right hand corner.
> ➢ Enclose return postage.
> ➢ You can submit to more than one publisher/agent at one time.

Poetry Magazines

The rules differ slightly from large-scale prose, so here they are in full.

> ➢ If you know the editor's name, use it.
> ➢ Print out your poems exactly how you want them to appear on the published page.
> ➢ Use a new sheet for each poem, and print on one side of the paper only.
> ➢ Double-spaced format isn't necessary and may mislead the editors with regard to your stanza breaks. Make sure any stanza breaks are obvious.
> ➢ Put your name and address at the bottom of each sheet in case your poems are separated.
> ➢ Send no more than six poems in any one submission.
> ➢ Try to avoid over-complicated layouts in your poems, as these can cause typesetting errors and/or spoil the movement of the poem on the page.
> ➢ Never send a return envelope which is smaller than A5...and
> ➢ Don't send the same poem to more than one editor at once. They will not be impressed if they see that another editor has chosen the same poem for publication at a similar time (and in the eventuality, will probably send you a note expressing their distaste). Moreover, poetry readers who pay high subscription fees to two or more poetry magazine do not wish to see material repeated between them.

You need a covering letter too; and that's all. Short story writers don't need to send as many as six stories; two or three to choose from will be enough. In addition, it's important not to bombard the same editor with repeat submissions, because this looks desperate. It is far better to spread your talents widely and have several submissions on the go with different outlets.

> **Study Tip**
> Don't forget to keep a list or a chart showing what goes where. You need to track your submissions in case a pattern appears, such as one sort of work being accepted every time, or the same piece being rejected. It will help you channel your abilities towards the right editors, and you will avoid sending the same submission twice to the same editor by mistake.

What Happens Next?

Once your package is ready, obtain a certificate of posting from the post office as proof that you've sent the work to the publisher. Some people recommend using recorded delivery, but this is expensive, and it can lead to uncollected works back at the sorting office when staff, absent at the time of drop-off, come back to discover a post-person's card on their desk rather than your envelope.

And then you wait. And wait. New writers have no idea just how much waiting is involved. As a rough indication, three months is nothing unusual. If you've heard nothing after eight weeks, send a polite enquiry to the publisher. This often produces a response, and if you are lucky, the publisher will ask to see more of your novel.

Poets and short story writers will be waiting a similar length of time. Some literary magazines have editorial meetings once a month or less; hence their slowness. If an editor is running a magazine on her own in her spare time, it's unlikely she can plough through the submissions and organise an edition in anything less than three months. I've often had to wait nearly a year before having a poem accepted, only for another year to pass before the poem is in print!

Exercise

At this stage, you should have some idea about where your first submission should go. Yes – it's time to stop worrying and revising – seize the day and join the published writers. Or not. You'll never know what might happen if you don't give it a try.

Take your best four to six poems or your best two stories, or your synopsis and first three chapters. Then package them up, insert your stamped return envelope, and drop them in the nearest postbox before continuing with the rest of this chapter.

Follow the advice given in the preceding paragraphs, and your work won't end up in the dustbin. Of course there's a lot more to the editorial process after a piece is accepted – but that's outside the scope of this book. You do, however, need to know how else you can promote your writing. Assuming that you have completed enough of it, two excellent options available to all new writers are: self-publishing, and competitions. Read on to discover more about these.

Conclusions

Most people who take up writing have an ambition to see their work in print as a final outcome. It's a laudable ambition, and there's no reason why it can't happen to you. With this in mind, prospective authors should study their market and know what the editors want. You should follow the recommended submissions procedures and be prepared to wait patiently while your work is processed. If your work is rejected, you should re-package it and send it to the next place on the list.

Tutorial Section

Points for discussion

1. Why do the rules for submission differ for poetry and prose?
2. Do you think script assessment services are worth the money?
3. Do you think a poem about a current event is still worth submitting to a poetry magazine, even if you know you may have to wait up to two years to see it in print?
4. Would you only be happy if your work was published by a player in the big press industry?

Practice Questions

1. Draft up a submission covering letter for the last piece of creative writing you produced.
2. Research script assessment services on the Internet and see what differences exist between companies.
3. Practice creating a synopsis by summarizing the last film you watched.
4. Search for several different poetry magazines on the Internet, and take note of their submission guidelines.

9 **Self-publishing and Competitions**

One Minute Overview

Acting on the advice in the previous chapter may have already led to your work being accepted by a major publishing house. However, there are ways other than submitting to editors that can still get your creative piece into the public eye. Self-publishing and competitions are big players on the contemporary publishing scene. The phrase "spending money to make money" will probably feature in your thoughts if you seriously contemplate either – but make sure that it is money well spent, and you aren't caught out by a scam artist. There are some out there.

Self-Publishing

Thanks to advanced software, this is now seen as a realistic alternative for writers. If your work is specialised or not commercially viable, or if you want a small print run to celebrate a local event, turn to the world of self-publishing. There's no mystery to it, and the end result will be similar to a professionally-managed small press book, providing you pay attention to the fundamentals.

There are a number of self-help guides which explain the process in detail, but the following information will start you off. It may be all you need for a short enterprise like a one-act play or a few poems.

> ➢ Have your book camera-ready – that is, typed and arranged exactly as it should appear in the published version.
> ➢ Don't forget the contents list, page numbers, and all the trappings which indicate it's a book.

> ➤ Cover design – try not to have a complicated one. A simple photo or line drawing will be easier to reproduce.
> ➤ Take your prototype round at least two printers and get an estimate for the total cost. Their addresses are in the Yellow Pages. Try to choose one who likes literary jobs as opposed to company handbills and leaflets.
> ➤ A printer is an expert, so listen to any advice he or she might have.
> ➤ Choose your paper and cover boards; the printer should have samples. Remember that non-standard sizes and heavier paper, special finishes, etc. will add to the cost.
> ➤ Standard print runs for self-published books are: 100, 250, and 500. You might only need 100.
> ➤ The printer will probably request a disk version of the text and a hardcopy.
> ➤ Ask for at least two proof copies, and then you can keep a check on the progress of your book.
> ➤ Allow up to three months for printing.

You can cut costs on small booklets by doing the collation (page sorting) and stapling yourself. A long-arm stapler is all you need; this will cope with 24-page poetry booklets. If your own computer is up to it and your printer is one of the advanced ones, you could even produce your own booklets on a 'print on demand' system, without using a commercial printing firm.

What about the ISBN?

You'll be aware that books normally carry an ISBN on the back or near the frontispiece and contents list. These are blocks of serial numbers allocated to publishers for use on each new book – and they come at a cost. As a self-publisher with maybe one book under this method and no others, it isn't worth your while applying for an ISBN. The number is nothing more than a location unit for distributors, stock-buyers and booksellers, yet the shops will be taking your book direct from you as opposed to ordering from websites, distributors, and catalogues.

If your aims are modest as a self-publisher and your market is localised, or within a specialist area, you can save some money by not applying for an ISBN. Furthermore, having a number is of little use when you have a booklet with a stapled spine, as the chain bookshops frequently don't stock anything other than flat-spined books.

Marketing

When the supplies arrive, you can think about publicity. Among your strategies you should consider these:

> Send a press release to the local papers and your local radio/TV station, telling them briefly what the book is about and who to contact. Enclose a review copy if you can.

> Send other review copies to any specialist journals or societies, with a brief note indicating that it's for the review pages.

> Finally, plan a reading or launch and sell copies on the night. Don't worry – there's more about events in the next chapter.

> Set up a website and mention the site on your correspondence.

Self-publishing is particularly useful for social historians, playwrights, and performance poets, since copies can be sold at talks and gigs. It's just as easy for novelists to self-publish, except the costs are much greater and it might be double the effort in terms of shifting copies afterwards. But let's look on the positive side: one or two novelists have been picked up by established presses as a result of good marketing after publishing their own work.

Wait a Minute – What's A Press Release?

Press releases are how many local journalists receive news, and they will often be the best way of securing a few column centimetres in the papers, or a piece of airtime with your local radio. Your employer may have a publicity or communications person who provides these on behalf of your office or industry. A good press release acts as a hook to generate interest and create a newsworthy story.

If you've never written one before, don't worry. Skilled publicists will know many artful marketing tricks, but a first-timer can write an effective piece too. Here's how:

> What they want is news, remember – first book, exciting murder mystery, new poet in town, rare research, unusual facts in print at last, forthcoming event.
> Provide the author's name, the title, any strong promotional statement about the work.
> If there's an original human interest angle you can provide, include it. Overcoming dyslexia, being told at school that you 'couldn't write', extremes of age .... all these hooks have been used to grab newspaper space.
> Give details about when the book will be published or launched, and where the reader can buy one.
> Have a phone number so people can contact the seller direct.
> Keep details sharp and to the point – no long elaborations on the themes, or explanations about your previous works. Your promotional statement and/or intriguing information should be no longer than a paragraph.
> Think of the typical journalistic rules when writing a press release: Who, What, Where, When.

Most of the above details will enable a journalist to construct a few paragraphs about your book. They may ask you for more background information (the How and the Why), which is where you provide the depth and detail which you couldn't include in the press release.

Study Tip
There's another handy journalistic rule, and it's KISS – Keep It Simple, Stupid!

Selling to Shops

Not as difficult as you might think. Firstly, forget about the big chains and high street outlets, since they don't accept self-publishers or small presses. Stick to owner-managed independents and localised chains. Also try:

> Local discount bookshops.
> Your friendly secondhand book dealer.
> The local museum and library, community centre reception area.

It's surprising just how many of these outlets will help a writer on the way, particularly if your material has some regional interest and you've used their premises during the writing period.

Ask to see the stock-buyer and leave them a copy of the work, with your contact details. They will need two figures: the selling price for them and their buying-in price from you, known respectively as the retail and wholesale prices. Check in a couple of weeks if nobody has got back to you.

Sale-or-return is when the bookshop takes a few copies, and returns them at no cost to themselves if any copies stay unsold. This is the usual deal you will be on, as a micro-press.

Always carry a few copies and a receipt book in your glove compartment, because you never know when a suitable outlet may arise. As a first-collection poet, I managed to place my work in a number of shops simply through approaching booksellers out of the blue.

Remember that the first six months after publication are the best time for placing your works in shops. Any longer than a year and your book is already old news. Make sure they're appearing on shelves while the year on your frontispiece is the same as the one on your calendar.

Where Else?

Self-published writers have successfully sold their works at crafts fairs and similar events. For a small cost, you can hire a table and sell your wares direct. Contact your local tourist information centre or council markets officer for the details of anyone who runs crafts fairs in your area. It's possible to hire a stand at a regional arts festival, and existing festival bookstands may let you add a few of your own works providing you collect them up at the end of the day. When trying for table space at a book festival, you must contact the administrators at least six months before the event, as otherwise they will have all been snapped up.

If you're running your own stand, become colour-coordinated and place your stock at different heights against a plain backdrop or tablecloth. What attracts you to a stall when you're a customer? A few flat books on a bare table won't do you any good. Why not wear an advertising T-shirt too?

Study Tips
Nobody wants a garage full of unsold books. The commonest mistake among self-publishers is: overestimating the print-run.

If setting up as a self-publisher, give the press a name. This will carry more credibility with shops. If you can't think of anything, trees or geographical features are a good bet. Some people use their road or house name.

Competitions and Prizes

Competitions are big business in the creative writing world. Some authors hate them, seeing the whole idea of selection and judgement as a mistake. Others think it encourages too many no-hopers into clogging up the system, while the prize money is handed out to people who might never amount to anything in the long run.

But competitions are extremely popular with entrants. They're democratic. You don't need to be an established writer, and since entries are judged anonymously, you don't need to be known by anyone. That's why they're ideal testing grounds for new writers who aren't yet ready for wider publication.

It's possible to be a total beginner and still do well in a competition. This includes you!

A commended rating can do wonders for your confidence, while being unplaced means you have probably shared the same fate as some well-known entrants. There's no bad outcome – and your work is soon released for the next competition or a magazine submission. Best of all, publishers often look at the major competition results lists for new talent.

Types of Competition

Unpublished novelists have only few to choose from. These include the Debut Dagger (for crime writers, run by the Crime Writer's Association), the Dundee Book Trust, and the Yeovil Literary Prize. Expect to be sending in a few chapters and an outline or synposis; and have a first draft completed in your stores, just in case.

Poets and short story writers have much more choice. Nearly every county has a competition run by an arts group, and many literary magazines have them too, with publication as part of the prize. Among the big players are the *TLS* (*Times Literary Supplement*), *Mslexia*, the Kent & Sussex Poetry Society, and the Bridport. Other organisations, which exist to promote writing in all its forms, will have a competitive fling every now and then – the Arvon Foundation runs its massive competition every two years. The 'National', run by the Poetry Society, is a popular yearly choice.

In addition, you will find smaller regional competitions like the Southport, the York Open, the City of Derby, and ones which are integral to festivals, like the annual Ledbury and Cheltenham competitions. Some are run as fundraisers for charity; the LACE was on behalf of Age Concern in Lincoln. A few small presses have yearly booklet competitions, which provide a great first move into print – Smith Doorstop is a reliable one here.

Outside the purely literary market, women's magazines occasionally run competitions. These are advertised prominently on the covers, so you won't have to look too hard. Apart from their large circulation figures, winning one of these might help with an entry into journalism.

What should you look for in a competition?

> ➤ Worthwhile prize money. It sounds obvious, but some have rewards which are unequal to the entry fees.

> ➤ A judge who is authoritative in writing or literary studies. Not the town mayor or a D-list celebrity.
> ➤ A judge whose works you know and enjoy.
> ➤ Clear concise rules, so that it's impossible to get things wrong.
> ➤ Publication as part of the prize.
> ➤ A few places for runner-ups, with a chance to be published with the prizewinners.
> ➤ A performance evening or anthology launch.

Where Do I Find The Entry Forms?

Libraries, colleges, arts centres, public galleries and local authority arts departments usually receive packs of leaflets about forthcoming competitions. Tackle the racks, and if nothing is there, ask the staff for information – they might have reference copies. Since all but the smallest magazines now have an online presence and good websites, it's possible to find out the latest details and download forms directly from the Internet.

If you're already on all kinds of mailing lists, you may receive some of the larger competition forms without having to chase them up. But it's better if you do the following. Subscribe to a couple of writer's periodicals, for example *Writer's News or Mslexia* (for women writers), and the journalists involved will keep you informed. You will also receive regular tips and hints, which will help you on your way.

At this point, it's a good idea if you stop reading, turn to the Internet, and look up the magazines in your genre. If they have free email bulletins and a mailing list, sign up and get yourself on their database. While you're at it, contact your regional arts council office and put yourself on their literature mailing list. They often send out quarterly bulletins, which include competition listings.

Not a net-head? Don't worry – collect forms of the competitions that interest you, and save them. They reappear at the same time each year, so make a note and send off for the next ones, enclosing a stamped addressed envelope. Friends sometimes post duplicate forms to me, and maybe yours will do the same. A day spent in London at the Poetry Library (part of the South Bank Centre near Waterloo) will enable you to track down competitions and the magazines which host them.

How To Enter Competitions

Believe it or not, some people pay no attention to the rule sheets when they forward their work. Their entries will be binned without delay. With hundreds of works to read through, the judges and preliminary sorters can't spend any time on entrants who refuse to play the game. It's not unusual for a third of the total submissions to be unreadable, crumpled, outside the catchment area or subject range, without return envelopes or addresses, or just too bad to qualify. Therefore, you can go further simply by following the instructions on the sheet.

- ➢ If it says double-spaced, print your work in double-spaced format.
- ➢ If it says 'do not put your name or address on the work', leave your works anonymous and put your details on the accompanying form, or on a separate sheet as instructed. Entries have to be judged without the writer's name being known.
- ➢ Avoid sending pleasant notes, pictures, or embellishments on the paper. All they want are: the entry form, the works, and the payment.

If the rules are ambiguous, there is usually an enquiry number supplied with the competition details or on the relevant website. It is far better to sound like a fool on the phone, rather than to misinterpret the rules and send your entry spinning into the paper-basket.

So that your work isn't tied up for months on end, forward your entries within the last month of the closing date. Apart from cutting down on the waiting time, your work won't be resting too long in that dead zone where you can't make any more submissions with the same piece. This is important for writers who are less prolific – one or two items may be all you have for a year's worth of competitions.

If you can track down a number of prize-winning works, analyse what common traits they share.

Schemes, Scams, and Vanity

In the Introduction, I mentioned expensive holidays and retreats which aren't always necessary for beginners. Most of them are perfectly genuine residential study weeks and they're taught by experienced tutors. And it might be just what you need, if you have a noisy family to escape from. But there are a number of specific scams, typically aimed at new writers, and you should be aware of them.

The main one to watch out for is the vanity press. These advertise in all sorts of periodicals claiming to be looking for talented new authors. When you send your manuscript in, you will receive an ecstatic report telling you how wonderful your work is, and that they'd love to publish it. The only problem is – you have to pay for the cost of publication. Naturally, desperate authors after years of rejection are only too happy to do this – and so are new writers who are unaware of the scam.

The company takes your cheque, and you hear nothing further. On enquiring about your book, you will find that nothing has been done about the marketing or distribution, and there is a box of shoddy, unsaleable-looking products in a basement somewhere which you then have to sell/get rid of yourself. Bookshops won't take the book, a) because the production isn't up to standard, and b) they can see it's from a vanity press.

Yet you paid up, and the contract looked all right – what went wrong?

Dohh!

You have fallen victim to a vanity press; so-called because they prey on the vanity of would-be authors who'll go a long way to see themselves in print. And, like the flu virus, they mutate into different forms to trap the unwary. Names change, they go out of business, and reappear a while later passing themselves off as new publishers. The vanity press is more likely to take poets, because the resulting book is cheaper to produce than a novel.

Ignore their pleasant and winsome advertisements. Genuine publishers never need to advertise for manuscripts, and genuine publishers never take money up front from you. A genuine publisher will take work and publish it at their own cost, and at some future date, you may expect a payment. Never pay a publisher to see your book in print. This isn't how it's done.

What Else?

Along with the vanity press, you might come across the vanity anthology. This is when a 'press' organises a competitive-entry publication, and you pay (for example) £5 to send in your work. Before the book appears, you are sent an order form to buy in your copies; naturally, these books are always overpriced and not up to the standard of a genuine small press. And the victims eagerly buy several copies to show their families and friends.

What's gone wrong here? Only that you've paid to send in your work … and then paid again to receive the book. Meanwhile, the 'press' has pocketed all those fees and amounts, with the actual book production costing them only a fraction of the amount they've received.

The problem is, writers who are taken in by this nice little earner are completely unaware that they've been scammed. They can't understand that they've appeared in little more than a vanity publication, which hundreds of people have paid to be in, and which has no artistic value beyond the circle of contributors.

I'd also look carefully at competitions and how they are run. Some are expensive to enter, yet the prize money is modest by comparison. They might not be paying a judge or holding a celebratory reading either. Question: where are all the cheques going? I'll tell you where. To the administrators who dreamed up the contest, of course.

Tread carefully if you are approached by a 'subsidy publisher'. These are a sort of half-legitimate version of a vanity press. You'll be spared the flattery, but you will be asked to pay up half of the publishing costs, while the publisher makes a reasonable attempt at producing a book. You'd still do better as a self-publisher. On the whole, subsidy products look dated and like nothing on the shelves at Borders. Many industry professionals regard subsidy publishing or partnership publishing as vanity work under another name.

And here's the latest thing. At the time of writing, 'print on demand' (POD) is making inroads into the small press and Internet publishing scene. Some of these operators involve authors paying for publication yet again – you have been warned.

Avoid Them!

To avoid scams and vanity presses, always check for the publisher's details in the *Yearbook*, the *Handbook*, or through your regional arts offices. The latter will know of reputable presses, which are too small to advertise in the handbooks. Some local authority arts workers have publishing enterprises in addition to their day jobs, and it's worth asking them for advice.

There is no substitute for being aware of the publishing scene in your chosen genre. Know who are the leading publishers, the intelligent small presses, the magazines, the websites. Subscribe to a few of them; send off for some of their catalogues and books. Look for reputable competitions and publishing schemes run by places you've heard of and local organisations you can trust. Accept nothing less, and you won't fall victim to a vanity outfit.

You might think I'm labouring this point about vanity presses. But the fact remains, despite warnings being in all writers' handbooks, innocent people continue to pay such outfits even though the book industry doesn't work like that. Caught-out writers will even say 'I know it's a vanity press, but …' as if they imagine there's some merit in it, or that they are the sole person who isn't a victim. Vanity presses are not the way into print for anyone who cares about literature, books, or publishing.

What is OK?

Small presses may request that you buy back a few copies of your book at the wholesale price and help with marketing. This is OK. Very small presses – one-man operations without the help of grants and sponsorship – may pay you in kind, such as giving you part of the print run. That's OK too. And self-publishing, where you organise everything yourself and pay a printer, is also OK.

A magazine may organise an anthology, and they ask your permission to include a poem or short story, which they've already printed elsewhere. After the book is out, you will receive a complimentary copy and an order form in case you want a few more. Or: you send in your unpublished work for a regional anthology, it's selected without cost to yourself, and you can buy the resulting book at the organised launch. You will often have a free copy sent in any case.

Editorial and reading services, where you are charged for a report on your work, are also acceptable. You can't expect a detailed report from an industry professional for nothing. Some critical services are run through regional arts council offices or the Poetry Society; these are reliable options.

> **Study Tip**
> Remember, if you can't get a publisher by the traditional route, turn to self-publishing and advertise your book on the Internet.

Extra: What Happens to Your Book?

If you're unfamiliar with the publishing process, here is a quick outline of what happens once a small-to-medium publisher has accepted your work.

1. You will receive a contract or agreement on paper. It might be a brief one-page statement if dealing with a community press; or a massive 28-clause monster if you are with a commercial concern. In it you should have payment details (royalty or flat fee), rights and responsibilities, and … one or two penalty clauses if you fail to deliver!

2. Complete your typescript within the deadline and submit it as requested. Standard procedure at the moment is two hardcopies and one disk version.

3. You'll have to supply alterations or rewrites if the publishing staff believe it necessary. Swallow your pride and do them – it's your first book and you want it out!

4. Your script may then go to a freelance copy-editor. This person crawls over every sentence to check for grammar and factual problems. You'll get a list of points for correction. Again, do them – the editor is probably right.

5. Your book goes into production. Layout, size, font, etc. will be decided. You'll receive proof copies before it goes to print, and you'll have to check everything with your master-copy again.

6. You might receive jacket designs, and there might be a choice if you're lucky. But it's normal for the publisher to do everything concerned with jackets. Yes, even if you're a Slade-trained artist and he's hiring his mother who can't draw.

7. Usually, authors are asked to supply a 'blurb': see below for information on this witty little item that can help move your work off the shelves.

8. The printer may take longer than expected – don't be alarmed if the book is overdue. This is normal. Try not to pester the publisher during this final waiting period.

9. On publication you'll receive a number of free copies, normally 6–10 unless another figure is mentioned in your contract.

10. You might have to share in some of the marketing – providing addresses, finding independent bookshops and local radio contacts.

The Lowdown on Blurb

Blurb is the promotional statement which goes on the flyleaf of your book, or the back cover. It's usually short, less than two hundred words, and it's intended to encourage the bookshop browser and 'sell' the work. You may be familiar with overblown hype-ridden blurbs which don't live up to expectation when you start reading the contents ....so make sure you are truthful as well as promotional!

Small presses with no marketing people (and even some larger outfits) will ask you to provide the blurb. Therefore, it's never too early to learn. How would you sell the following books?

a) The Bible.

b) A report on the current state of Britain's gas-pipe manufacturing industry.

c) The trendy biography of a leading fashionista, written by a close family friend.

You may be asked to provide a line or two about yourself, so compare how other authors describe their achievements. An easy solution is to cite your main qualifications and a relevant job, or a previous publication. Here are two different statements, showing how authors might display their experience:

Emma Bovarie is a renowned breeder of Pekingese dogs, living deep in the French countryside. This is the first installment of her searing autobiography, one written after undergoing extensive therapy in Vienna.

Charles Heckmondwike has an MA in Cultural Studies from Bradfield University. He tutors for the Open University and co-edits the Journal of Contemporary Discourse. He is currently working on his second collection of poems, Straws in The Wind.

The first example is clearly about someone who has little writing experience, but she might just have an intriguing human interest tale; the second is someone with a career angle to his writing, who is advertising himself as a scholarly fellow as well as a creative writer.

If you experiment with self-publishing in the future, a good blurb on the back cover will help your work to cross the boundary. It will look more like a real book, and less like something produced in your spare time for personal reasons.

On Your Side

If you're worried about the contractual side of things, you may be eligible to join the relevant unions like the Society of Authors or The Writer's Guild once you have published a few items. The Society of Authors has a contract-reading service and many problems can be solved before you sign your time away on the dotted line. The Writer's Guild is traditionally the one for script and media-based writers. I would strongly recommend joining one of these professional associations if you intend staying around as a writer, or alternatively, if you are managing your new career without an agent.

Don't forget, if you run into problems with your script, like: difficulties at home, computers crashing, losing the typescript on a bus, an inability to write it … tell your publisher sooner rather than later. Publishers are not the enemy – they've invested time and money in you and they would rather see the book in print. On the other hand, bad or impossible projects can be brought amicably to an end providing you are honest and polite with it.

Conclusions

Remember that no reputable publisher will advertise for manuscripts.

You should have considered that some competitions are expensive to enter, yet the prize money is modest, and it is arguable that the only 'real winners' are the administrators who dreamed up the contest.

You will have discovered that an excellent blurb on the back cover could make all the difference in the world of self-publishing.

You've hopefully learned to be honest about problems if you can no longer work co-operatively with others on the publication of your work.

Tutorial Section

Points for discussion

1. Why shouldn't people use a vanity press if that's what they want? Hundreds of willing subscribers can't be wrong.
2. Do prizes and competitions alter the nature of people's work, or change what becomes acceptable to editors?
3. Why are there so many literary competitions, most of them for poetry?

Practice Questions

1. Investigate your options for publishing on the Internet, starting with some of the website suggestions here in the bibliography.
2. Write a hundred words of promotional 'blurb' for your current best work.
3. Devise a 16-page A5 sampler showcasing your work, using the formats and layouts you would expect to find in a published booklet.
4. Write a press release promoting the above work.

One Minute Overview

Now you're writing regularly and there's a file of works in your drawer. You have plans, and you know more about the business of writing. But it's a bit solitary sometimes – you could do with some like-minded people. Not everyone wants to write in secret. And it takes a very long time for publication to happen, so you need a few opportunities along the way. Joining in ensures you'll have some social benefit ... and marketing ones too. If your work's good, word will get around and you'll become known as a writer. Here are some solutions to that marketing problem, and how to remain in contact with the outside world.

Classes and Courses

Creative writing is such a popular pastime that a whole industry has grown up to support this modern phenomenon. There are heaps of courses, ranging from no-qualification ones to those giving transferable credits towards a degree. Naturally, they're not all using the same model. If you need something more substantial than a drop-in workshop, research your options.

Which, What, & Where?

Local courses generally start in January or September, with brochures available at libraries, tourist information centres, and community centres. Some courses may allow entry at different times during the year. In addition, there may be separate workshops run by arts centres and County Councils who employ tutors as part of an arts development programme.

Look out for courses run by Lifelong Learning or Continuing Education departments. These will be attached to a regional university, often hiring the same tutors. In the case of Lifelong Learning departments, you don't need qualifications to join their writing courses. These options can be researched through the main university websites; if you can't find the URL, try the university name followed by '.ac.uk'.

If you live in a rural district where nothing seems to happen, it's worth writing to your county leisure or arts officer to see if provision is being made. You may also find tutors advertising workshops in new age and alternative therapy centres, church halls or community-run cafes. If you are already writing a lot and a certificate isn't necessary, a few workshops are probably all you need to keep focused.

Can't go to a regional college? Here's something designed for you – there are online writing sessions and home study correspondence courses. The latter are run by organisations like the National Extension College and the Open College of the Arts. You can study online with Manchester Metropolitan University, and also Nottingham Trent. Carers and others who are tied to a home environment often choose these options, and certificated courses often have message boards, forums and opportunities to meet others face-to-face during the year.

Get Yourself Organised!

If you are thinking of starting a course or attending a few workshops, collect brochures of the ones available in your area and begin to compare. Consider these points:

- ➤ Does the course cover all the topics you need?
- ➤ Is it affordable? Are there hidden extras? (Such as course books, subscription fees etc.)
- ➤ Is the course run by a recognised academic organisation?
- ➤ If not, is it run by a local authority, the Worker's Educational Association, an arts organisation, or similar?
- ➤ If neither of the above, is it run by a published writer with a teaching certificate?

> ➢ If not a writer, are they at least someone with a background in editorial work or publishing?

If it offers none of the above, forget it.

There's no point in being taught by someone who is unpublished, or lacking a recognised teaching qualification. They probably don't know any more than you. Always check the credentials of anyone who sets up to teach – if you meet with refusal, cross them off your list.

Checking for a teaching certificate (B.Ed., Cert.Ed., PGCE or a current adult education equivalent) will guarantee a basic level of professionalism and experience. Also, if the tutor is a writer, it's worth finding out when their last book was published. If more than ten years ago, it's likely that they're not currently engaged in the writing scene and their information may be out of date.

Course fees vary tremendously, and in the case of tutors running individual workshops, much will depend on the cost of room hire (which the tutor is responsible for). A safe rule: if it sounds like too much for a couple of hours, it probably is.

Despite some of the caveats about unqualified and non-writing tutors, joining a class is one of the best ways to develop as a writer in a supportive atmosphere. You'll meet like-minded people and make some good friends. In addition, there are usually publishing and performance opportunities thrown in: look out for courses with a yearly anthology, website publishing site, or an end of term reading. And you might have a natural organiser in your class who is only too happy to fix up trips to events.

Complaints Department

When starting out, I attended all kinds of workshops. Some of these were taught by people who regarded the job as money for old rope. They would roll in, plonk an object on the table, and tell us to write about it for half an hour. I was inexperienced, so I didn't complain. But I knew I was learning nothing, and that we weren't being taken seriously. If you feel there's no structure to a workshop – maybe the guy just rambles on about his difficult life and reads from his deathless prose – mention it to the organiser. This isn't how you learn to write. As a minimum outcome, you should be taking away a half-finished draft or a list of ideas.

Colleges and adult education centres will usually have an official complaints procedure. If raising matters with the course organiser has no effect, try the head of department or director. Avoid personalised comments though such as 'he obviously hates me', and stick to the facts: things which can be proved or agreed by other class members, like: 'our work is never marked when it's been handed in' or 'she's always half an hour late'.

Courses often conclude with evaluation forms. Take it from me, the staff really do follow up on the suggestions made. If all of the students say too much time is spent on dishing out photocopies, the papers will be issued in packs as you enter the room instead. But course problems can only be sorted if students write down what's bothering them!

Many courses have a cut-off limit; after a certain date your deposits and course fees aren't refundable. If you leave within a couple of weeks, you can probably get your fees back. Check any cut-off dates before requesting, and drop out sooner rather than later.

Clubs, Groups, and Societies

The Writers' Group

While courses proliferate, writers' groups are also hugely popular. You can find the addresses of local contacts at libraries, arts centres, and with arts staff attached to County Councils. There is probably one near you. However, you may need to try more than one before settling in: some groups fossilise early on and become cliquey. Aim for one which meets on public premises rather than in someone's front room. It's harder to be critical if you're sitting in someone's best armchair while enjoying their hospitality.

Check that your potential group has some of the following:

> ➤ A chairperson and/or secretary.
> ➤ Meetings once or twice a month.
> ➤ Regular manuscript nights where members read and discuss works in progress.
> ➤ A willingness to offer constructive criticism, not: 'yes, very nice, dear' or 'it's not quite my kind of thing'.
> ➤ A website and webmaster to look after it.
> ➤ Annual anthologies/a competition.
> ➤ Occasional guest speakers or visiting writers.
> ➤ Workshops and writing time.
> ➤ More than five members.

In short, the group should be active, welcoming new people and attempting to help the existing members with advice. It helps if they have links to an arts centre or annual festival, if they hold a reading night every now and then, if one or two members have enjoyed publishing success, whether it's in free newsletters or a novel on sale in Waterstone's.

It helps if someone in the group is skilled at networking, or prepared to have a go at raising funds from local sources and the National Lottery 'awards for all' schemes. Some of the better-off groups produce their own anthologies and publications. These won't have a wide market beyond friends and family, but they provide a good publishing credit for beginners.

Since writing is often seen as a solitary occupation, published writers often pour scorn on the idea of a writer's group. And it's true that coming across a clique-driven one is counter-productive for anyone learning the trade. In particular, members might exist all on the same 'level' creatively, having no tolerance for the person who turns up with an outrageous piece of sci-fi or a literary chapter which is well beyond the understanding of the Chairman. If this happens to you, move on. It helps if a group understands a wide range of writing styles.

At its best, a group will provide a friendly and supportive environment for you to progress with your writing. You should hope to be writing a further item for the next meeting, and you should hope to hear about competitions and other opportunities. If none of this happens, leave.

Try to avoid:

> ➤ Groups with members having 'issues' – drugs, depression, psychiatric disorders. They'll spend most of the time discussing their problems.
> ➤ Groups with dictators in charge (including benevolent dictators).
> ➤ Groups where one person is seen as the star and everyone else isn't; because if your work is good, they won't want a rival.

Yes, it's a mixed bag out there. But at the very least, you can obtain lots of character material.

Remember you are dealing with personalities in a group situation, and it isn't the same as a taught class where you can expect a structure and a set of outcomes.

The Reading Group

Like writing groups, their makeup and organisation can vary depending on who is in charge. Typically, they will meet once a month and discuss a book which the members have read during the previous weeks. In working over a notable piece of fiction, you'll realise more about the nature of writing and the techniques used by the selected author. Group members will come up with creative and stimulating ideas that you won't find in critical books and official biographies.

Libraries and regional arts officers will have the contact details for local groups; some large firms and office blocks have reading groups too, encouraged as part of a staff welfare programme. A reading group is ideal for someone who finds it difficult to share their unfinished writings with others, but who nevertheless wants a social angle with literature.

The Literary Society

Interested in a specific author or poet? They probably have a support society. There's one for nearly every major writer; sometimes more than one. Sherlock Holmes has his own, even though he doesn't exist. New ones start up when a dead writer is discovered to be popular, or is rediscovered through a new biography and/or a TV series. You can check them out in the Writer's *Handbook* or *Yearbook*. Some societies deal with groups of writers and a few relate to specific geographies; the Friends of the Dymock Poets and the Mary Webb Society being two examples.

If you love a specific novelist, there's nothing more involving than spending a weekend with a bunch of enthusiasts as you walk the landscape and listen to talks given by leading authorities. It's artistically rewarding if you learn about that author's particular techniques, what kept them going, how they overcame rejection. If you are researching an author, I would recommend joining the relevant society – often, you will find material which isn't widely published or known about.

The downside is you may meet more than your fair share of cranks. Sad, but true. Some societies take ownership of the author, and dismiss the opinions of any writer whose views don't correspond with those of the local established expert. It's fun to watch the in-fighting among the committees and even funnier when you meet members who claim to be a reincarnation of the author. There's nowt so queer as folk.

On the positive side: a society exists to promote its subject, which means newsletters and journals, if not books and pamphlets. They need volunteers to run the quarterly news-sheet, and people to review recent books about the subject area. Usually there's no payment for any of this (most societies are run on a shoestring) but it is valuable experience. A few years' worth of journal editing is a credit worth having if you want professional experience.

Furthermore, if you've carried out any original research, you have a readymade publishing opportunity in the next journal; or maybe a pamphlet to be included in the next mail-out. These routes are good entries for a novice writer.

What Should You Look For?

When choosing a literary society, look out for the following:

> Membership over 200 – so it's able to fund a few exploits.

> ➤ A constitution – chair, secretary, treasurer, AGM's and voting procedures.
> ➤ Nationwide membership – for diverse opinions and lasting interest beyond the home area where the author lived.
> ➤ A newsletter and journal, or a combined version of these, at least twice a year.
> ➤ Sponsorship of publications and/or events.
> ➤ A weekend of talks and study days.
> ➤ Social events (may be combined with the above).
> ➤ The involvement of descendants, biographers, archivists, educators.
> ➤ Ambitions: more members, republishing out-of-print books, publicity, a festival.
> ➤ A positive approach towards volunteers: i.e. they might want you on the committee, and not just for stacking chairs or buttering scones.
> ➤ Willingness to pass around information and addresses among members.
> ➤ Female? Watch out for old-school sexists. Yes, you'll be buttering the scones while some gormless chap meets the famous guest.

If the society has difficulty in providing information about itself and there's no clearly stated programme for the year, don't join. They won't be up to running events or publications. Even if you are joining just because you admire an author's works, you should expect one or two ways of improving your own.

It's also a good idea not to stick around if the same one or two people do all the talking / organising / publishing / promotion / research. It means you'll have to wait until they die before you get any writing opportunities. You can't wait that long.

Community Arts

Your district or town may be fortunate enough to have a community arts unit or similar. This is typically a public-funded unit of skilled workers, usually based on arts centre premises, who specialise in such areas as: after-school clubs, adult education, urban regeneration projects, and improving participation rates in the arts. Sometimes they are employed to run festivals and other celebratory events. Volunteers are always needed! Check with your local arts centre or town hall enquiry desk and find out what applies to your area. You may be pleasantly surprised.

Joining with a printmaker or music worker on a locally-targeted project will give you valuable experience. Songwriting, giant poster-poems, oral history and scriptwriting are all areas where you could offer something as a writer. It's unlikely you will be paid in the first instance, but it gets you a foot in the door as regards contacts and being noticed as a writer who likes to communicate.

Bear in mind that if you assist on anything to do with children or vulnerable groups in the UK, you will have to complete a CRB (Criminal Records Bureau) form and wait for clearance before you start. It's in your best interests to do this, because once you start working with public-funded organisations and teachers, your actions are accountable to the project managers. And you're unlikely to be hired in future unless you've been CRB cleared.

Festivals

There's a wide selection on offer every year, with vibes ranging from conservative to cutting edge. You are sure to find one that suits. In recent years the largest festivals have become commercial and oversized, setting the reader further apart from the author on stage. But it's one sure way to learn tons about the art of writing while having a holiday. Most festivals are in attractive 'tourist' parts of the country; Devon, the Suffolk Coast, the Welsh borders, the Lake District, St. Andrews, and Gloucestershire, to name a few areas. There are major city festivals in Birmingham, Manchester, Edinburgh and Lincoln, not to mention London. New ones climb onto the bandwagon, while some stay dormant for a couple of years. There is probably a festival within fifty miles of your address.

Here, you will find talks and workshops about what's happening now in literature: hip and glossy authors straight out of the Sunday supplements give meaningful talks about their latest works. Yes, it's a lot to do with fashion, and the tickets can be expensive for 'hot' authors. But you'll have a super-duper weekend if you've never been to one before. Look for any all-in tickets – they work out cheaper than buying for separate events. The organisation Ways with Words, based at Dartington in Devon, is a reliable provider of lit-fests around the country.

Poets have at least four specific festivals to choose from, at Ledbury, Southwell, Aldeburgh and Wells-next-the-Sea in Norfolk. You will find other festivals dealing with specific areas, like crime writing (Harrogate). Workshop places book-up fast, so get in early. It's a treat to be taught by great writers whose works you've admired from a distance.

Performing and Entertaining

As a result of belonging to a class or group, you might have a performance opportunity. If you're lucky, this could amount to a yearly allocation at a festival, billed as the local writers' evening. Or there might be a poetry slam at a fashionable venue, with an established MC/performance poet at the helm. Usually, a public reading might coincide with the launch of an anthology, or a publication from an unrelated author who needs more of an event buzz.

Regular stand-and-deliver open mike sessions can be found on the pub circuit; look into student bars, pubs with live events such as folk music nights, arts centre cafes, community-run cafes and the 'alternative' scene. While these events are nearly always for performance poets, they might have beginners' nights – but be prepared for heckling or the gong!

How to Read In Public

If you've been reading out sections of your work each month and nobody's fallen asleep or stuck their fingers in their ears, you can probably carry off a ten-minute slot without messing it up. Therefore, when the prospect of a performance happens, relax. Let's suppose you are about to take part in an event – say, a literature'n'pints session in a room above a pub. What should you do?

Here are some reliable rules for a pain-free reading session.

> Print your piece in a larger typeface than normal, in bold. Most likely you will be standing up when you perform, the page will be further away than it usually is, and the light will be dim.

> Highlight any words where you tend to stumble, giving you chance to think before you speak. If you mix up characters by mistake, put instructions in the margin like: 'this is Billy, not Jane'.

> Rehearse your piece several times. Not in the few minutes before the event starts. Read at a moderate pace, and test your audibility.

> Try to vary your tone of voice. Don't be a droner – the low humming noise will switch the audience off and the only thing they will remember was 'she was boring'.

> If it's a small room there won't be a microphone; if large … better test the mike and know what height you want it to be.

> Keep your pages in order with a clipboard or a ring binder. Messy papers look amateurish.

> To prevent turning over two pages instead of one, put coloured post-it notes with numbers on at the edge of each sheet.

> Keep introductions short – they shouldn't be longer than the work.

> Wear something flattering and clean. I'm sure that geniuses can get away with looking like derelicts, but the rest of us can't. Stained nylon shirts and faded purple velour jumpsuits give the wrong impression.

> Too much jewellery will distract the audience. They should be looking at you, not your earrings.

And finally:

> Never (and I mean never) overrun your allotted time. If the organiser says you have ten minutes, make sure your piece lasts ten. Those who overrun are not popular with the remaining readers, whose time is cut down thanks to you. And it's truly pathetic to come across the person who won't give up – I've seen poets with minders tugging at their trousers in a desperate attempt to make them stop. Don't be one of those!

Now it's time to look at what works best in performance for you.

Prose writers

As a general rule, it'll have to be a self-contained excerpt; a dialogue or four-page scene-setting episode; perhaps a short chapter introducing one character or showing your hero in a typical situation.

It must be understandable for what it is, independently of the whole story you are telling. Maybe you already have a short story which fits the average 10–15 minute reading slot. The audience shouldn't be left wondering 'who are these characters' or 'where is the scene taking place'. You shouldn't have to spend the first five minutes explaining the background.

Poets and dramatists

It's slightly easier for you, since there's an actual market for performance poetry. But this genre does have its own styles and preferences. On the whole, an introverted or lyrical style will fail, because it's meant for the page and not the stage. In fact, there's a big difference between a reading and a performance poetry event. One tends to be traditionally literary, whereas the other is noisier, younger, more brash and immediate – and terrific fun!

What Is a Performance Poet?

A typical performance poet on the circuit tends to be extroverted, politically inclined, and closely linked to either comedy or music. Some of them perform as characters. If you choose to do that, invent a performance persona that isn't too far away from your real character. Reason? You'll find it difficult to keep up unless you're a real actor as well. Rant, ingenious rhyming, social criticism and politics, tales from the edge; all these make good performance subjects.

As an alternative to the full-on performance scene, there are folk clubs and storytelling festivals. If dialect verse and accented country humour is your thing, there is a thriving genre of heritage and storytelling which you can join. Smaller festivals around the country will often take a chance on newcomers, and it's worth checking to see if there's a 'fringe' fest comprising of new performers and people giving it a go for free.

If you don't know anything about performance poetry, listening to the following pioneers will give you the picture: they all have CDs and published collections.

John Cooper Clarke
Joolz Denby
Mr. Social Control (also known as Will Holloway)
Jean 'Binta' Breeze
Attila the Stockbroker
Ian McMillan
Patience Agbabi

Sometimes, performance opportunities are advertised as a 'Poetry Slam'. This is basically a timed competition, where the best or most striking performance wins. It can be intimidating for new poets, so try the less competitive readings and open-mike sessions first. Find out how it happens by joining the audience at a festival-based slam.

Now Select Your Work

With some of the previous paragraphs in mind, look through your completed works and select what you might turn into a performance piece. Bear in mind the average ten minutes: as a group reader or inexperienced performer, this is your limit for a while! Look for:

➤ Strong characters who bounce off the page.
➤ Easy-to-follow sections of plots.

> ➢ Visual imagery, not abstract notions.
> ➢ One extended idea or comparison that the audience won't lose.
> ➢ A lead-up towards a climax or punch line.
> ➢ A piece which allows a varied tone of voice.

Once you have selected a couple of pieces, rehearse them as though you were taking part in a performance.

> ➢ Try it in front of a mirror first – look at your posture and attitude.
> ➢ Hold the papers or file firmly in both hands.
> ➢ Look at where the audience would be and fix on a point just above their heads. (Looking directly at faces can distract inexperienced readers at first.)
> ➢ Recite using a kitchen timer or alarm clock.
> ➢ Rehearse enough times so that you can remember some of the sentences without looking at the paper. That's when you can make eye contact with your audience or fixed point.
> ➢ When you are ready, drag a few willing victims into your orbit and test it on them.
> ➢ Listen to their honest criticisms.

Refining Your Performance

Record one of your performances and play it back. Listen critically – could it have been more interesting? Don't worry about accents, lisps or weak 'r's. You're not auditioning for a theatre company, and your accent is good wherever it comes from. But here are two things you should cut down, because they will affect your audibility at a distance:

> ➢ The glottal stop, as in missed out 't's: saying si**in for 'sitting', ge**in for 'getting'.
> ➢ Run-together words: *worralo*a* for 'what a lot of', *core snot* for 'of course not'.

Sentences full of the above will be harder to understand, although they can be useful for incidental characters and comic effects.

Writing Practice

Having a few performance poems up your sleeve might advance your case as a participant at events. Best of all, you don't need an abstract, 'poetical' mind to write one. The elements of performance verse can be boiled down to a few basic points, which anyone can try.

Think for a few minutes about what a performance poem should be like. What do you want to see and hear on the platform? Now write down what subjects, styles, and inclusions you want. You might have points like:

> ➢ Not too many metaphors – direct and forceful.
> ➢ Build-up and repetition.
> ➢ Phrases which the audience shouts out when you indicate.
> ➢ Insult verse, praise poem – ancient traditions.
> ➢ Big obvious puns which the audience can groan at.

Try this. Write a rant-verse about someone or something you really hate. Builders! Traffic wardens! Supermarket queues! The list is pretty long for most people. Throw in as much bile as you can. Use rhyming slang, exaggeration, patter, street language, argument. In the world of social comment and satire, everything is larger than life and twice as unpleasant. If you can't write as yourself, invent a persona who would be only too happy to say the outrageous things which aren't 'you'.

Remember some of the practice episodes from earlier on. Conversations, notes made in public places, good put-downs and one-liners; they might be relevant.

You will still need to edit and improve your work – if you're rhyming and scanning, remember that you can't get away with rubbish just because it's easier to understand. Listeners are often discerning and they'll recognise lame versifying as quickly as the page reader will. Use bad rhyming as a comic feature, not as an unintentional one.

The next time you attend a writers' group manuscript evening, read out your poem. Note down the reactions.

Running an Event

Perhaps you live in that area of the country where nothing happens, and yet there are writers who could join with you in a reading. Why not run your own event? Assess the quality and range of your local premises, and follow this set of straightforward guidelines. You don't need to be a go-getter to achieve a successful evening – all it takes is a little advance planning.

Sign up your readers and allocate their time slots. If possible, bring in a known writer or nearby journalist as the main attraction. Some don't charge any fees if they're local. A surprising number of authors are easy to get on with, and they relish a selling opportunity even if it's in a scout hut with a rickety table.

Allow about one and a half hours for the event, with an interval of fifteen minutes.

Choose a good MC – someone with a bit of dramatic flair and a carrying voice. They provide any intros needed at the start, for the main reader, on behalf of shy participants.

Join forces with another group if possible: this will automatically double your audience in terms of their friends and family.

If you're hiring premises, make sure the ticket price will recover costs on a smallish audience. You might not get a large audience for a literary-style reading … anything over 20 people is good!

Tickets on the door are easiest – selling them through another box office means you'll have to pay them commission and then wait a few weeks for the cheque to arrive. Alternatively, take reservations over the phone or by email. This has the advantage of letting you know how many people are interested, and whether you should do some more publicity.

Organise at least three months in advance:

> ➤ Your room hire: check the toilet and refreshments arrangements.
> ➤ Publicity targets (simple ones, like: libraries, local papers, local radio, colleges).

> ➤ Potential audiences, gathered through word of mouth and letter.
> ➤ Your box office – a mate with a cash tin on the night? Advance sales managed by one of the group?

Organise at least two weeks in advance:

> ➤ An entry for the local paper events column (listings are free in most regional papers).
> ➤ An A4 sized poster for the local library, tourism office, college, bookshop, newsagent, public building, corner shop, leisure centre.
> ➤ A rehearsal or two – particularly if you're working with unknown writers.
> ➤ Interval drinks – never leave your audience without access to refreshments or a toilet.
> ➤ …. and get someone in the group to take a few photos.

If it's a success, write a piece for the local paper and organise another event in six months' time. Whole festivals have begun from seeds like this.

Go for it

Now, think about the sort of premises which might be available to you. An arts centre room is obvious, but it might not be the cheapest option. Rooms above pubs, redundant churches, school halls, community centres, a garden marquee, museums and art galleries, bookshops; all these are possible. Some libraries provide premises hire, and some local authorities have community librarians who are only too happy to facilitate book-related events.

List your best local options with the contact details, and keep it for future reference. Bear in mind that a weekend of literary events will need a year's worth of planning – but a single reading can be achieved in three months and with one organiser.

Don't forget to visit some of the smaller regional book fairs, where you can pick up useful tips on what to do and how to manage your own event. Some organisers are willing to share contacts and hiring details, and you will also learn about what not to do; for example, scheduling your poetry reading for a time that a (noisy) children's workshop will be taking place in the room next door.

Conclusions

Writing is done by individuals and it's a great life for those with the determination to succeed. But it doesn't mean you have to be isolated or cut off.

In the early stages, belonging to a group will enable you to see the road ahead more clearly. A group may be important to you if your everyday life is not supportive.

Joining in with your fellow writers will bring all-important contacts, mutual support, and even a few writing or publishing opportunities. You will learn good tips and workshop exercises on the way.

The small press world is where many writers spend their careers. You have to be mutually supportive in order to keep up with events and find the available outlets. Some people imagine that the world should come to their door; in practice, it's the other way round. You won't be discovered unless you are prepared to meet your audiences half way.

Final Study Tip

Many historic writers' homes are open to the public, and among those which give a literary high are the Bronte Parsonage at Haworth, Keats' house at Hampstead, Dylan Thomas' boathouse at Laugharne and Thomas Hardy's childhood home near Dorchester. It's not just cheesy tourism. Seeing where writers lived and worked is often a visual stimulus and an inspiration to new writers. You might even come across people who like looking for writers' gravestones, or fictional locations based on real places.

Tutorial Section

Points for Discussion

1. How do you feel about sharing your unfinished works with others? How do you react to criticism?
2. Do you think that literary societies are a support or a hindrance?
3. Some literary festivals have musical events, cookery demos, and unrelated fringe performances. What does this tell us about the idea of a literary festival?
4. What other benefits may arise through attending a reader's group as opposed to a writer's group?

Practice Questions

1. Where are the storytelling and heritage outlets in your region? Check out the number of opportunities for live readings.
2. Experience the difference: read a traditionally literary poem aloud, followed by a performance piece or an extract from a play.
3. Write a convincing press release for a writers' group event.
4. Which other cultures have a thriving spoken word culture? What can you learn from them?
5. Look up the Internet site www.bookcrossing.com. Here, you can join a worldwide scheme for sharing literature with others. It involves leaving books in public places for strangers to find. The books are provided with serial numbers and you can track their progress around the country. Take a work you no longer need, and release it into the wild under this scheme.

That's All, Folks

You've now completed this manual and immersed yourself in starting to write. I hope it's confirmed your interest in writing well, and provided you with lots of useful information. You might need genre-specific guides next, and other works providing greater depth on areas that you're not sure about. Some of these guides will be available in the Studymates series.

Happy writing!

✳✳✳

Bibliography

Astley, Neil ed., *Poetry with an Edge*, (Bloodaxe, 1988)

Astley, Neil ed., *Staying Alive*, (Bloodaxe, 2002)

Bell, Julia and Magrs, Paul, *The Creative Writing Coursebook*, (Macmillan, 2001)

Blake, Carole, *From Pitch to Publication*, (Macmillan, 1999)

Casterton, Julia, *Creative Writing: A Practical Guide*, (Palgrave, 2005)

Dorner, Jane, *The Internet: A Writer's Guide*, (A & C Black, 2000)

Doubtfire, Deanne, *Teach Yourself Creative Writing*, (Hodder & Stoughton, 1983)

Finch, Peter, *How to Publish Yourself*, (Allison & Busby, 1997)

Grubb, Penny and Reah, Danuta *Writing a Textbook*, (How To Books, 1997)

Hilton, Catherine and Hyder, Margaret, *Getting to Grips with Writing*, (Letts Educational, 1995)

Jellicoe, Ann, *Community Plays*, (Methuen, 1987)

Laurence, Janet *Writing Crime Fiction, Making Crime Pay* (Studymates Writers Guides 2007)

Lynn-Schmidt, Victoria, *45 Master Characters*, (Writer's Digest Books, Ohio, USA, 2001)

Oke, Michael, *Writing Your Life Story*, (How To Books, 2001)

Oliver, Marina, *Writing Historical Fiction*, (Studymates Writers Guides, 2006)

Smith, Nancy, *501 Writers' Questions Answered*, (Piatkus, 1996).

Sorenson, Sharon, *How to Write Short Stories*, (Macmillan USA, 1994)

Stein, Sol, *Solutions for Writers*, (Souvenir Press, 1999)

Stillman, Frances, *The Poet's Manual and Rhyming Dictionary*, (Thames & Hudson, many editions)

The Writer's and Artist's Yearbook (A & C Black, yearly)

Turner, Barry ed., *The Writer's Handbook*, (Macmillan, yearly)

Turner, Barry, ed., *The Writer's Handbook Guide to Writing for Stage and Screen*, (Macmillan, 2003)

Wade, Stephen, *Writing Performance Poetry*, (Straightforward Publishing, 1998)

Walker Kate, *Kate Walkers 12-Point Guide to Writing Romance* (Studymates Writers Guides 2008)

Wetton Steve *Writing TV Scripts* (Studymates Writers Guides, 2005)

Writers at Work (the *Paris Review* Interviews, 5 vols. Secker & Warburg/Viking Press Inc.)

Useful websites

www.applesandsnakes.org (for poets)

www.artscouncil.org.uk

www.artsfestivals.co.uk

www.arvonfoundation.org

www.bbc.co.uk/writersroom/

www.booktrust.org.uk

www.britishcouncil.org

www.dundeecity.gov.uk/bookprize

fwwcp@cwcom.net (the Federation of Worker Writers and Community Publishers)

www.greatwriting.co.uk (fiction website and advice)

www.ireland-writers.com

www.lapidus.org.uk (literature and personal development)

www.literaryconsultancy.co.uk (for script assessments)

www.mslexia.co.uk (for women writers)

www.nawg.co.uk (the National Association of Writers' Groups)

www.ndc.demon.co.uk/als.htm (the Alliance of Literary Societies)

www.newwritingnorth.com

www.poetrybusiness.co.uk

www.poetrysociety.org.uk

www.pulp.net (fiction website)

www.rna-uk.org (the Romantic Novelists' Association)

www.scottishbooktrust.com

www.scriptonline.net

www.spreadtheword.org.uk

www.survivorspoetry.org.uk (poetry and mental health)

www.theatrewritingpartnership.com

www.thecwa.co.uk (the Crime Writers' Association)

www.theshortstory.org.uk

www.watch-file.com (for locating copyright holders in literature)

www.wayswithwords.co.uk

www.writernet.co.uk

www.writersbureau.com

www.writersnews.co.uk

www.yeovilprize.co.uk

Also try county and district council websites, where you will find tourism initiatives and festivals which relate to writing. These can be obtained by keying in the county or district followed by .gov.uk.

Useful addresses

The Poetry Library
Fifth Floor, Royal Festival Hall
The South Bank
Waterloo
London SE 8XX

The Society of Authors
84 Drayton Gardens
London SW10 9SB

The Worker's Educational Association
Temple House
17 Victoria Park Square
London E2 9PB

The Writers' Guild
15 Britannia Street
London WC1X 9JN

Scottish Arts Council
12 Manor Place
Edinburgh EH3 7DD

The Welsh Academy
3rd Floor, Mount Stuart House
Mount Stuart Square
Cardiff CF10 5FQ

Index